Hana Berger Sculpture

Published by: Yotzrim Art Gallery - Consulting and selling art
Design: Roni oz

© All rights reserved to Yotzrim Art Gallery - Consulting and Sale of Art- 2020
www.yotzrimgallery.com

Address: PO Box 5123, Herzliya, ZIP Code 4649719
Phone: +972-54-5286808

Do not reproduce, copy, photograph, record, translate, store in a database, transmit or receive in any way or transmit data from it in any form or electronic means, optical or mechanical or otherwise - any part of the material in this book. Commercial use of any kind of material contained in this book is strictly prohibited without the prior permission of the creators of the gallery.

Hana Berger
Sculpture

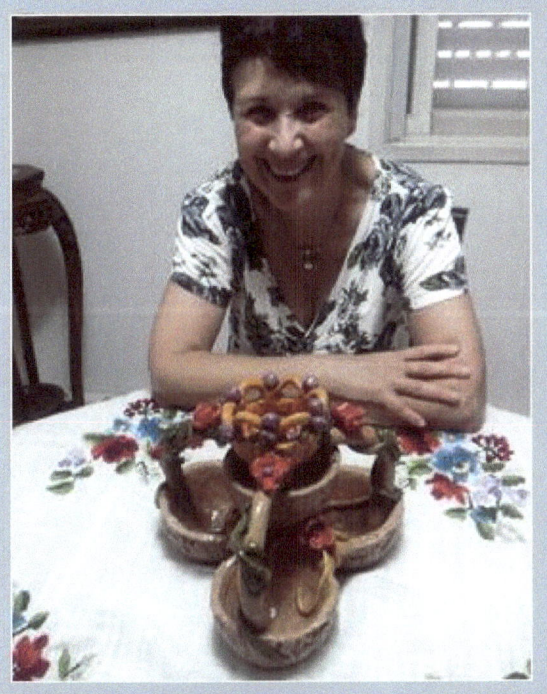

When I take a lump of unmolded clay in my hands, most times, I have no idea what I will ultimately create. A story slowly emerges as I work the clay, as I watch the shapes and colors form, as though I am communicating with the clay. This is **my** story.

My sculptures are usually abstract and colorfully painted.

Today, in my home, I am surrounded by many stories, and I am happy that I have found a way to express them through clay and color.

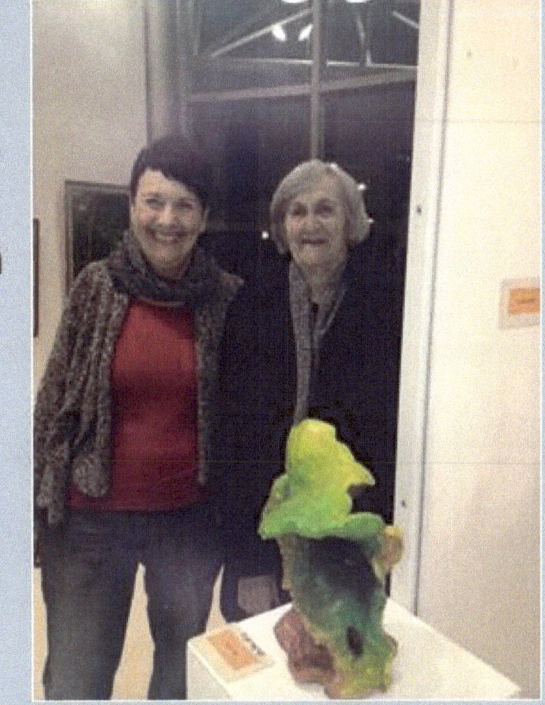

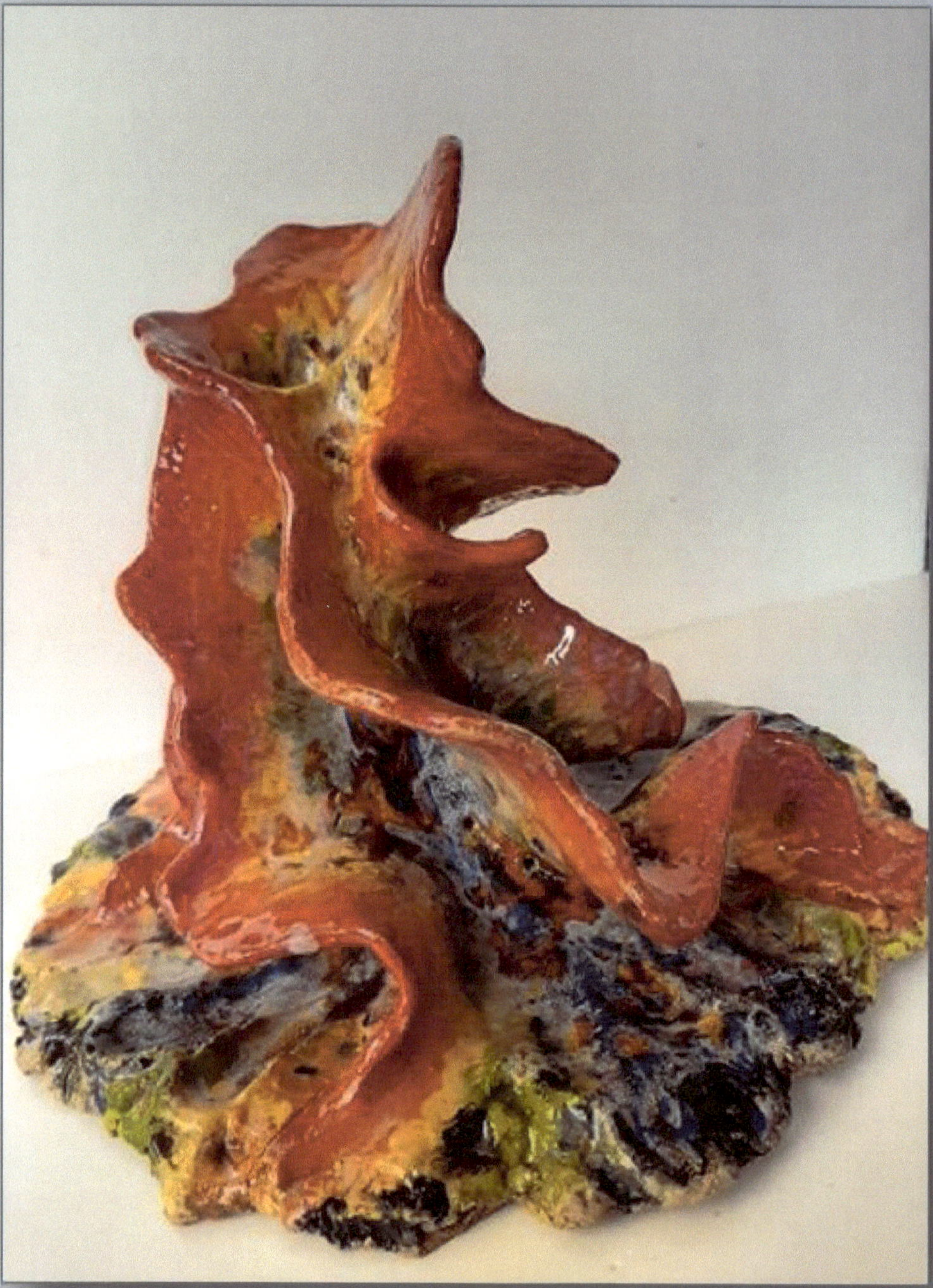

2021

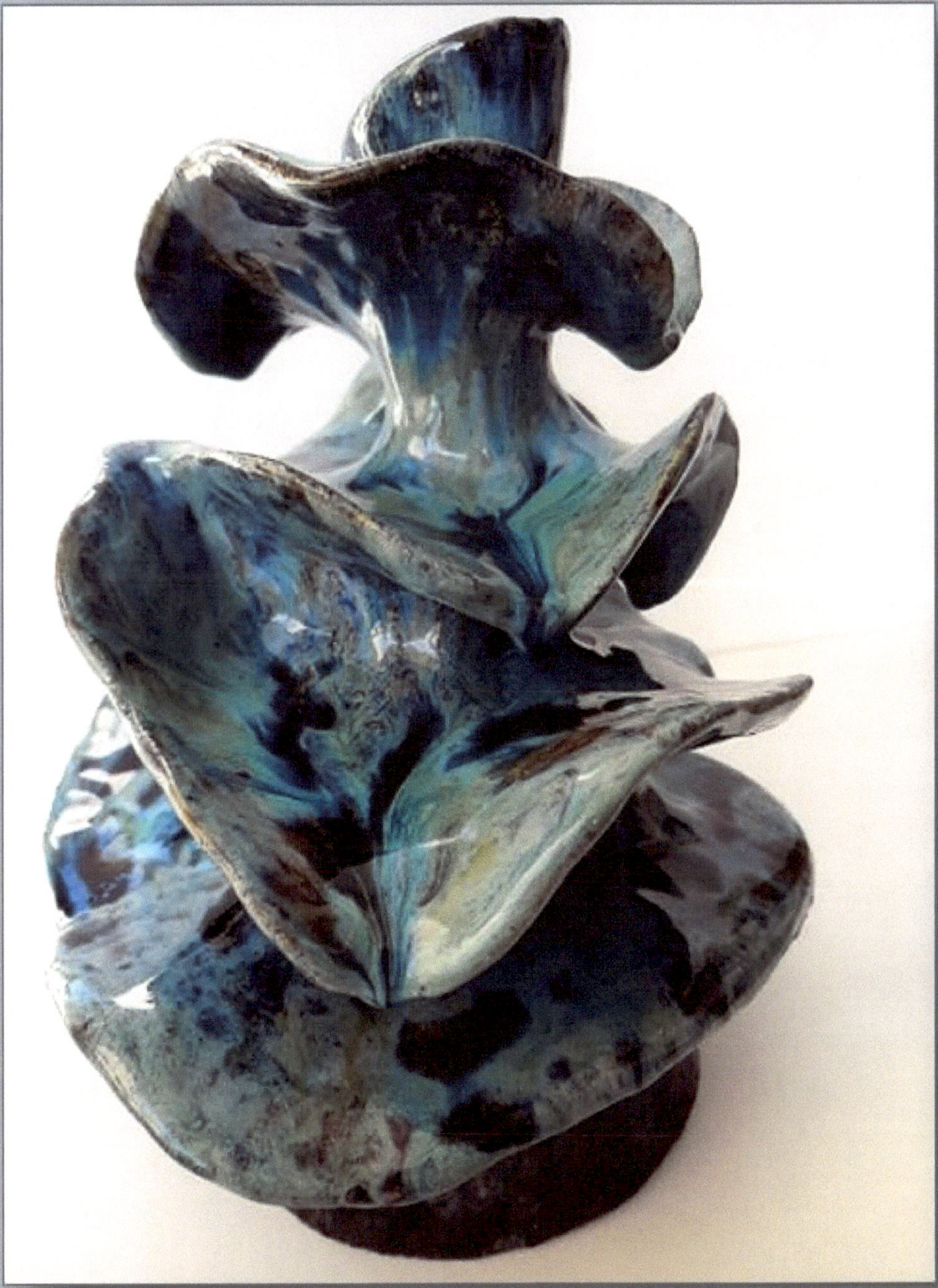

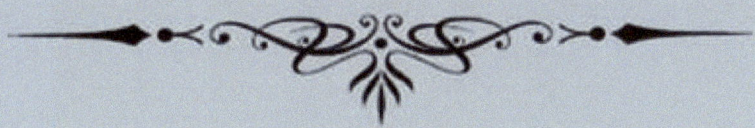

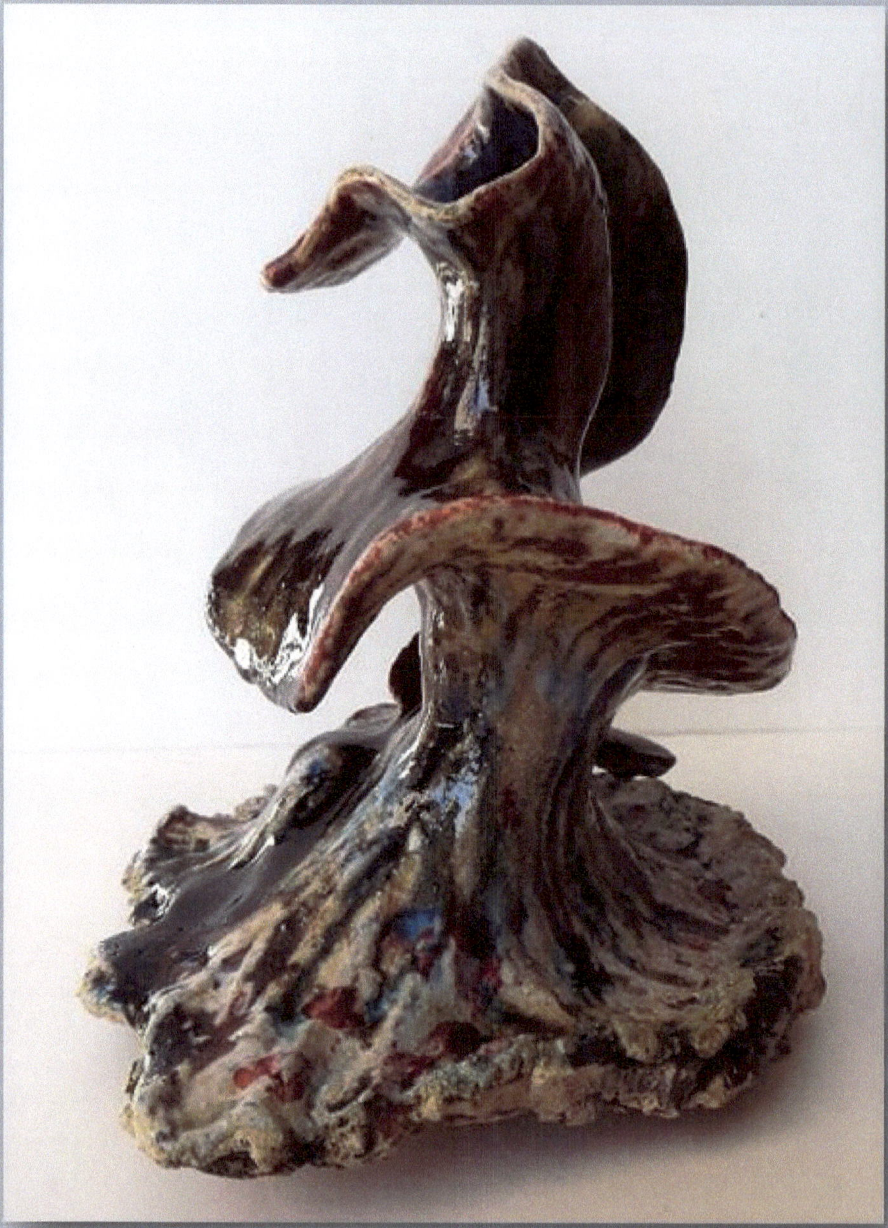

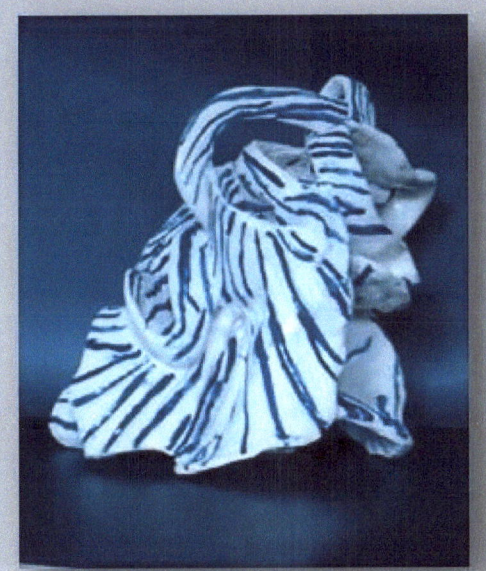
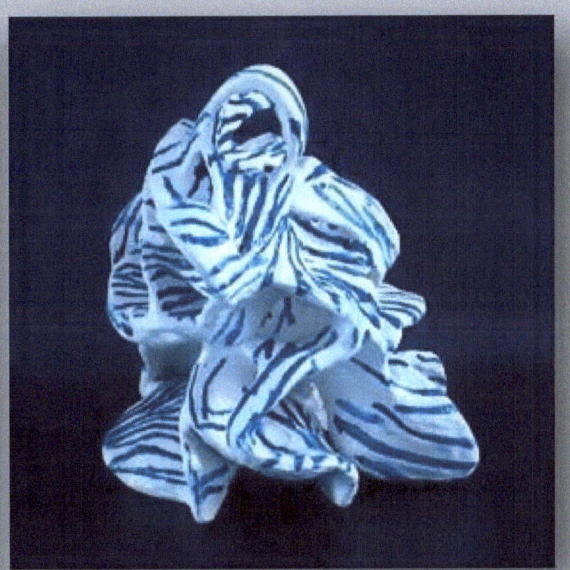
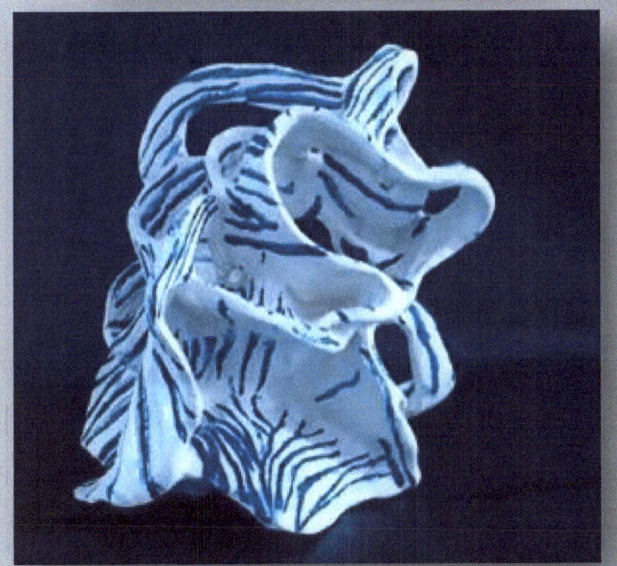
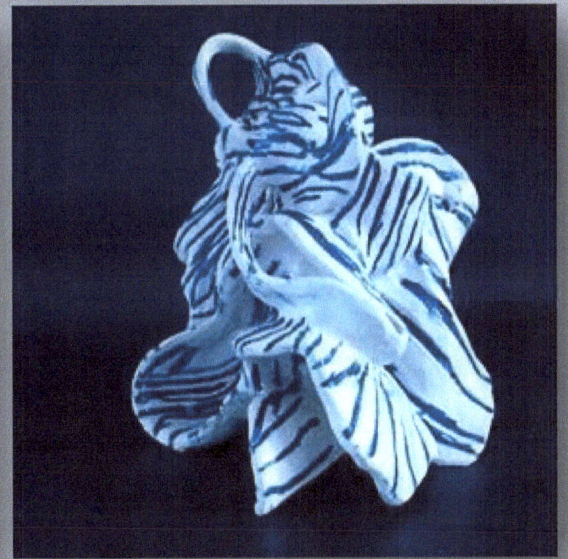

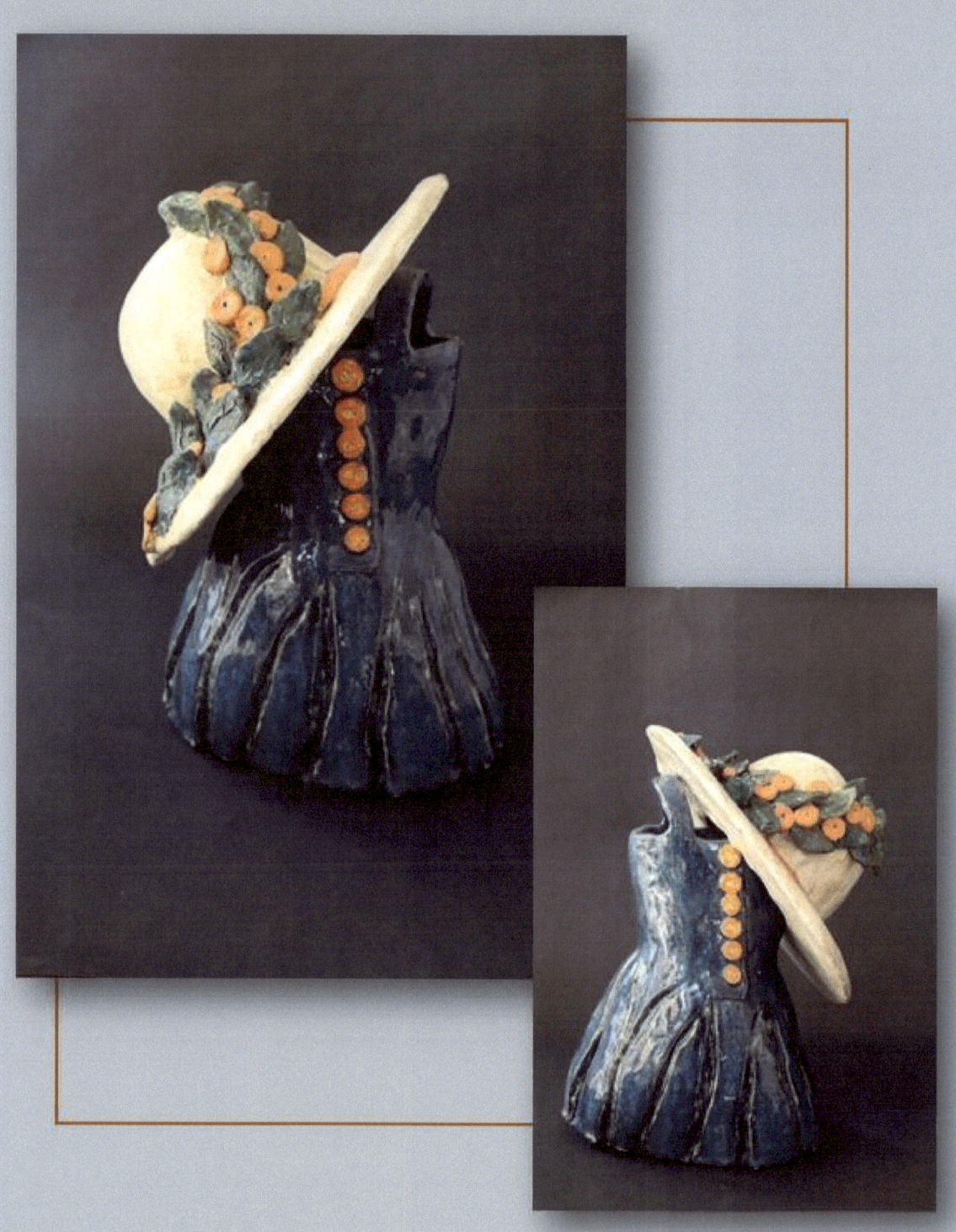

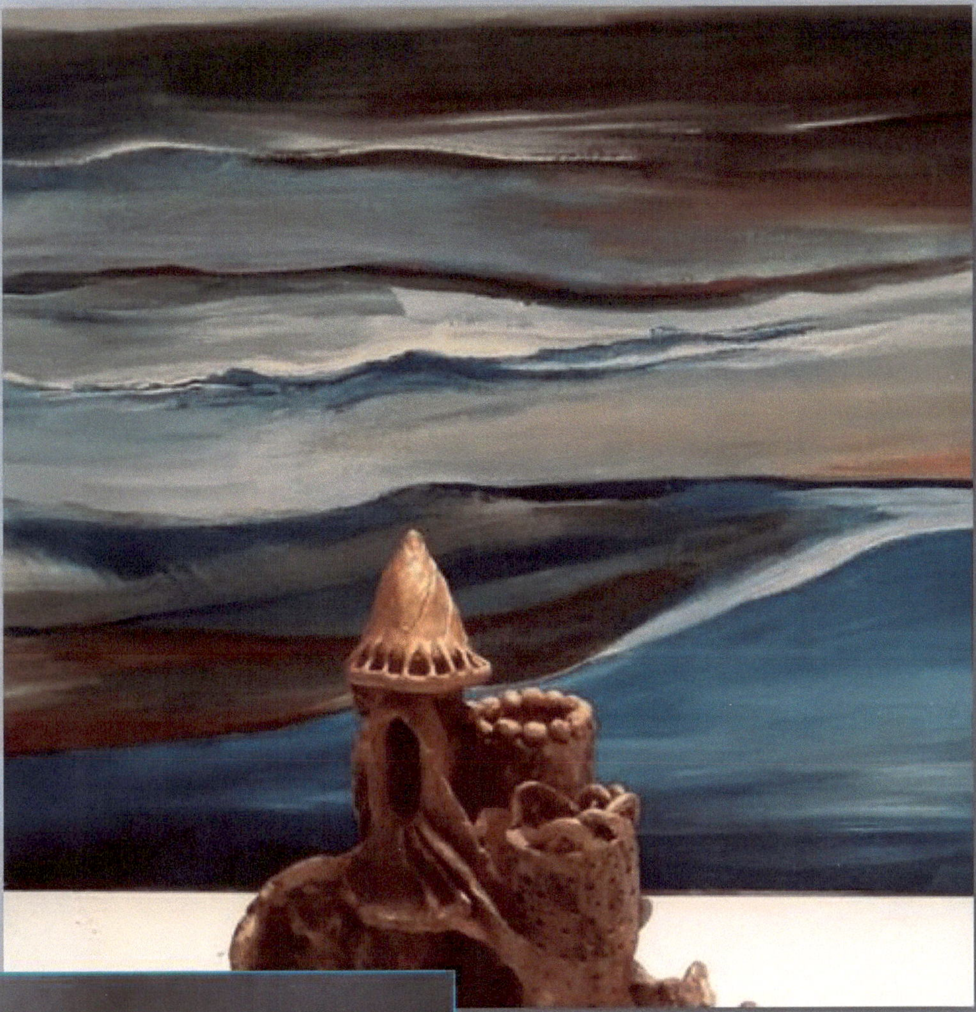

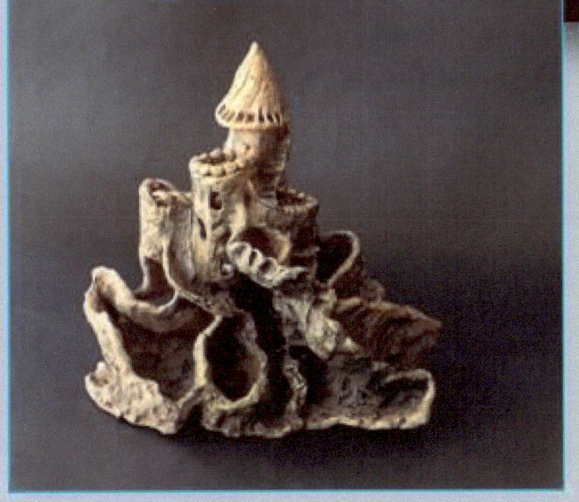

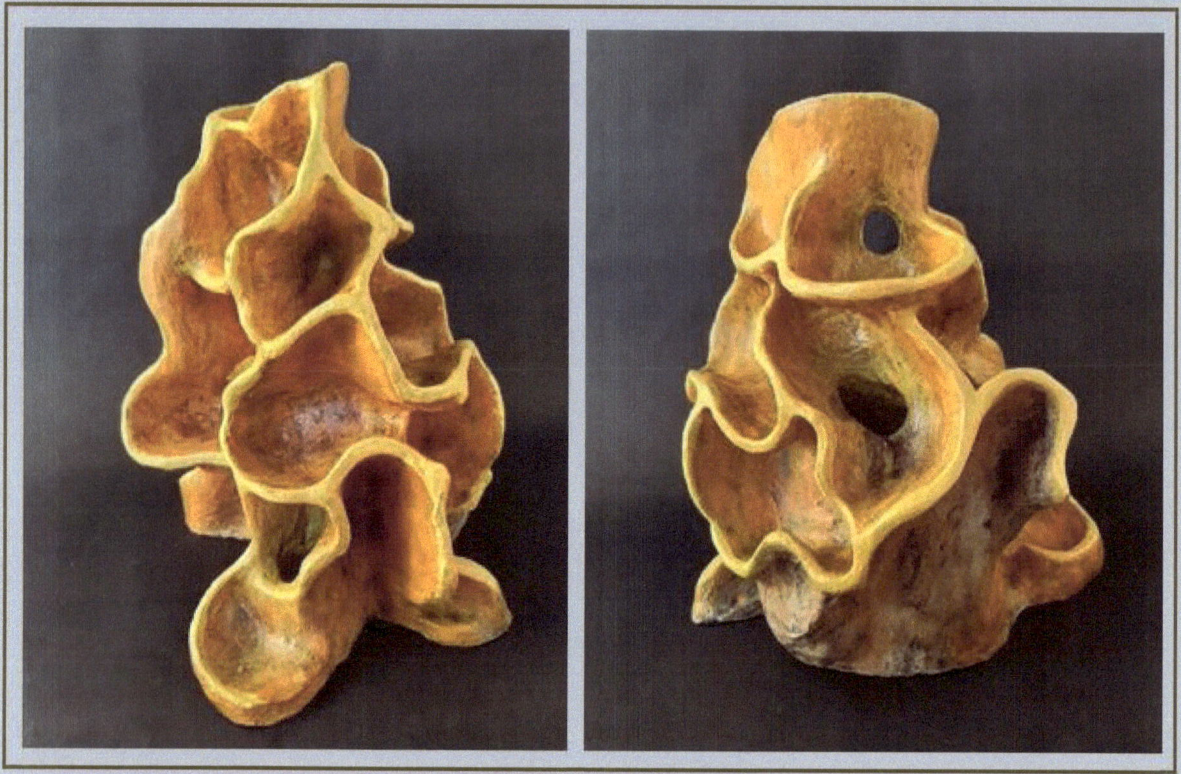

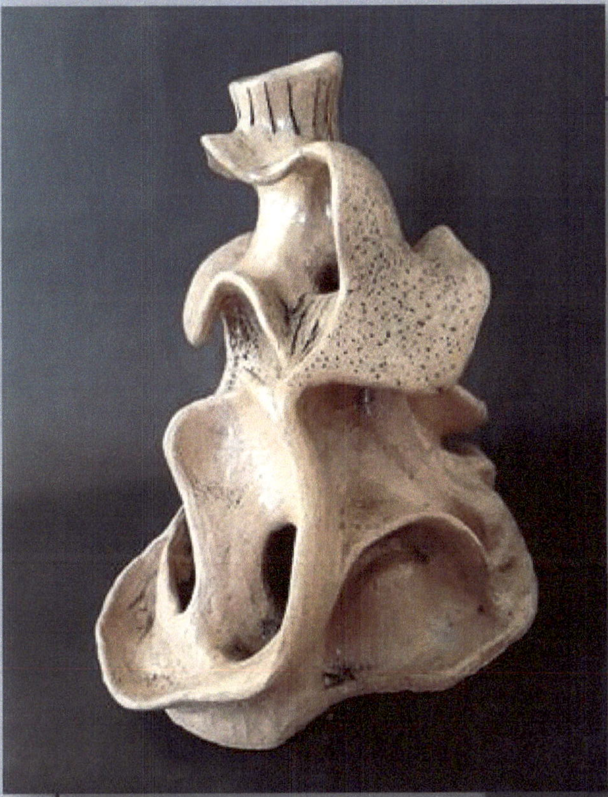

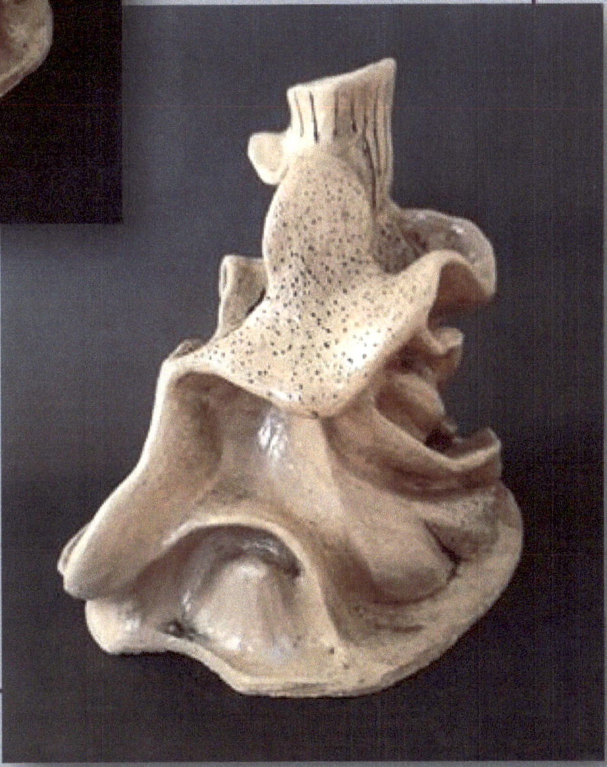

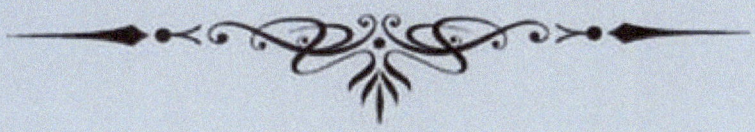

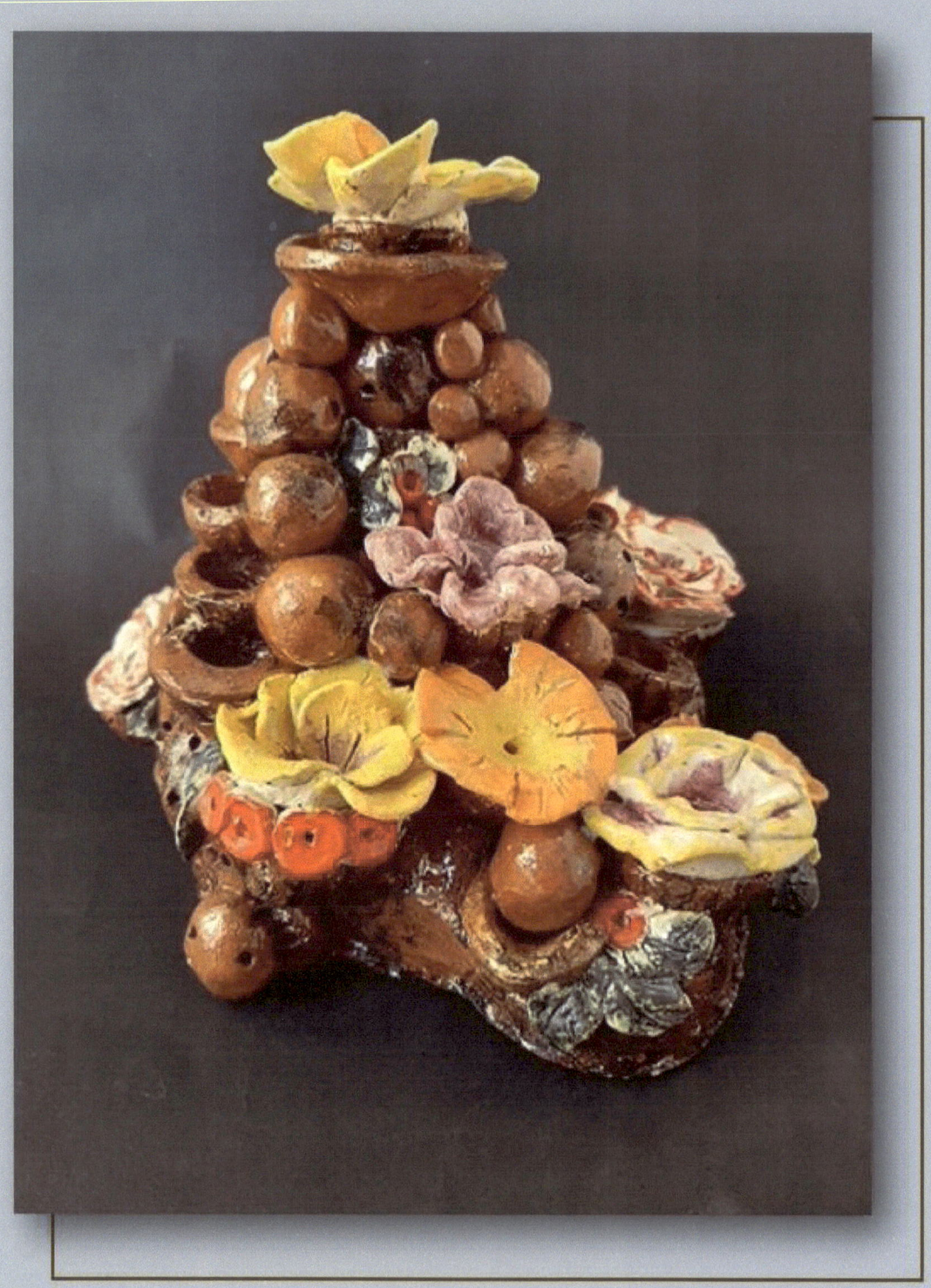

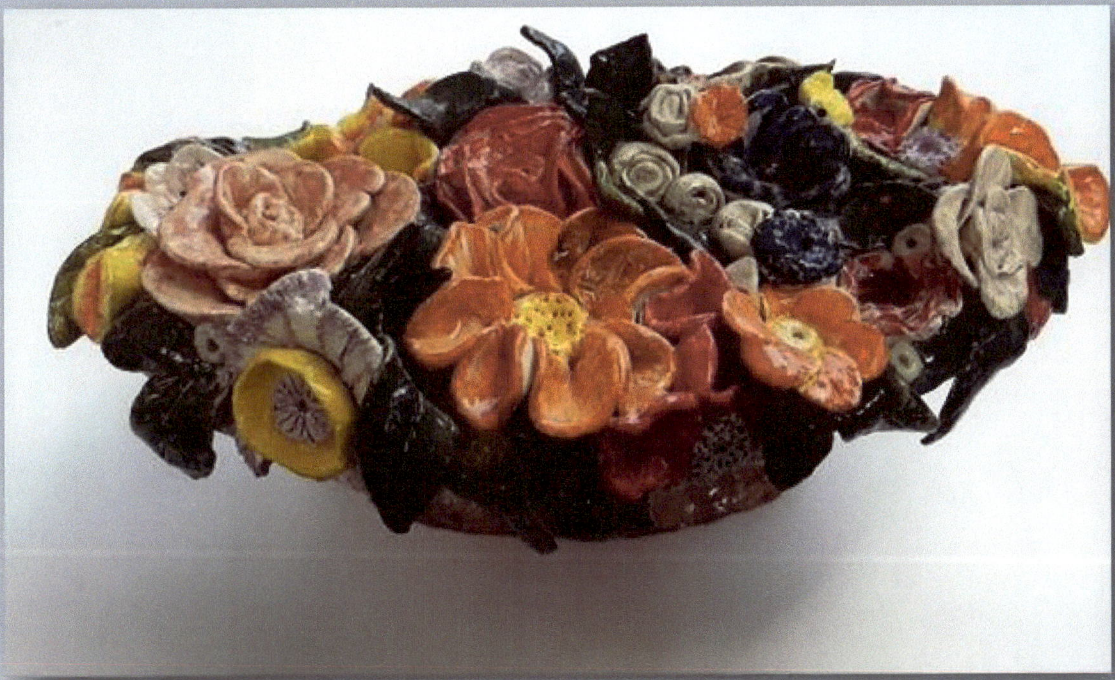

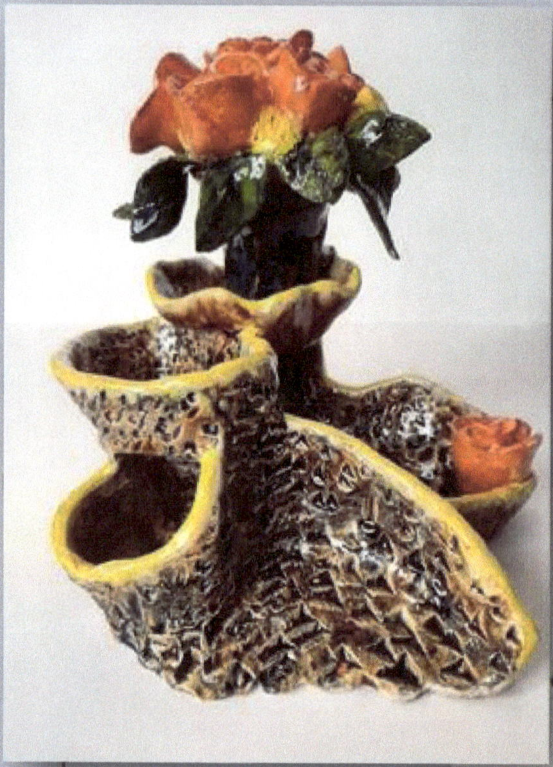

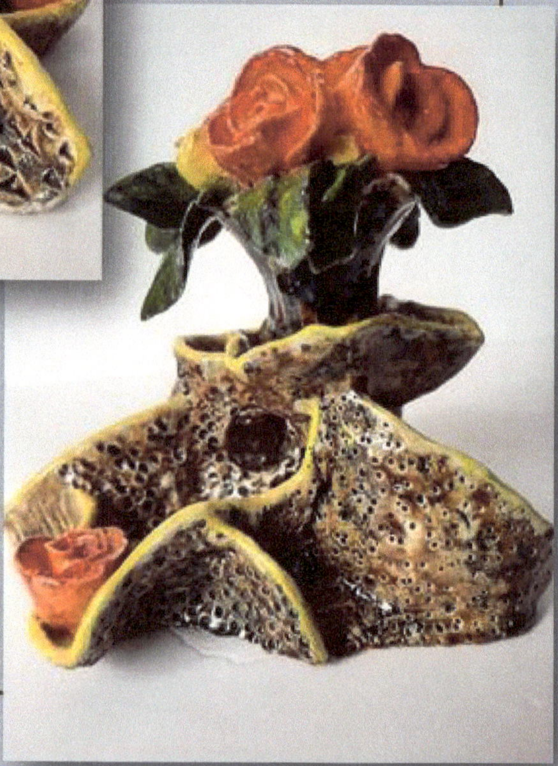

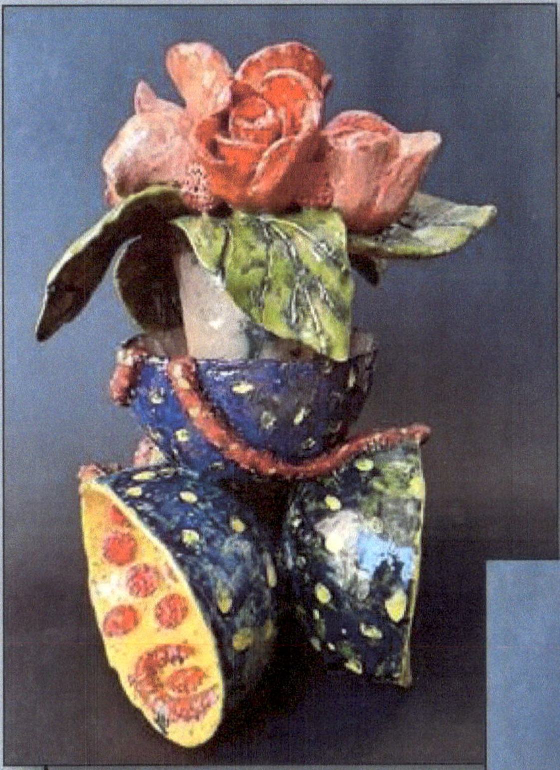

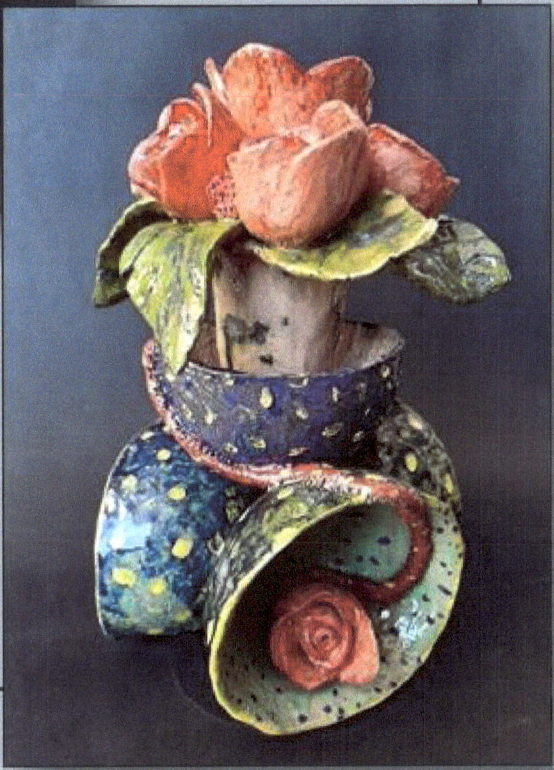

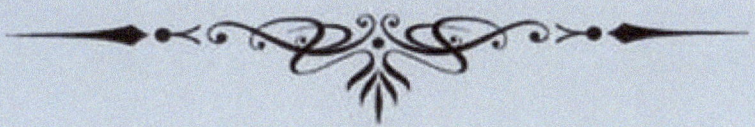

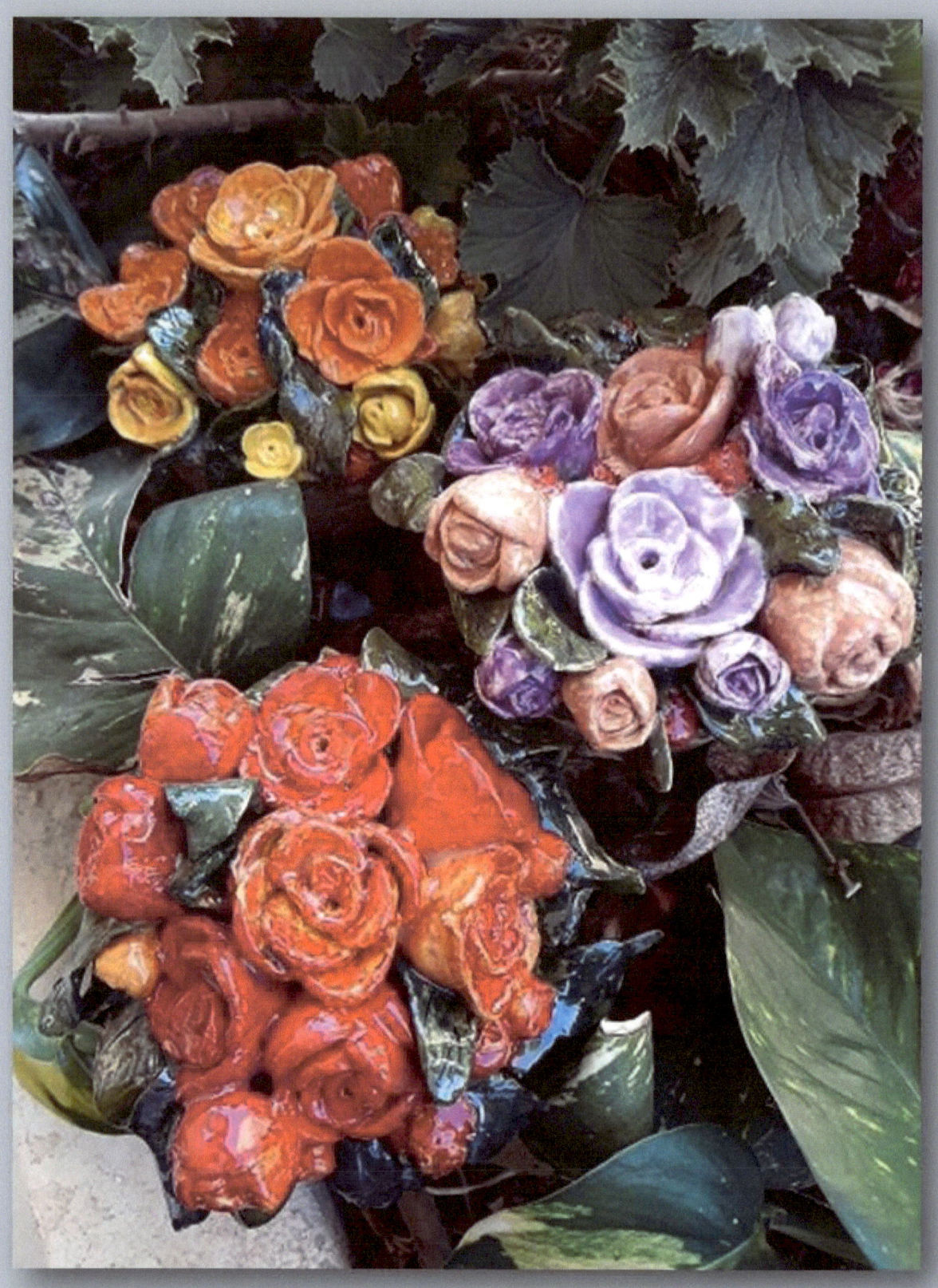

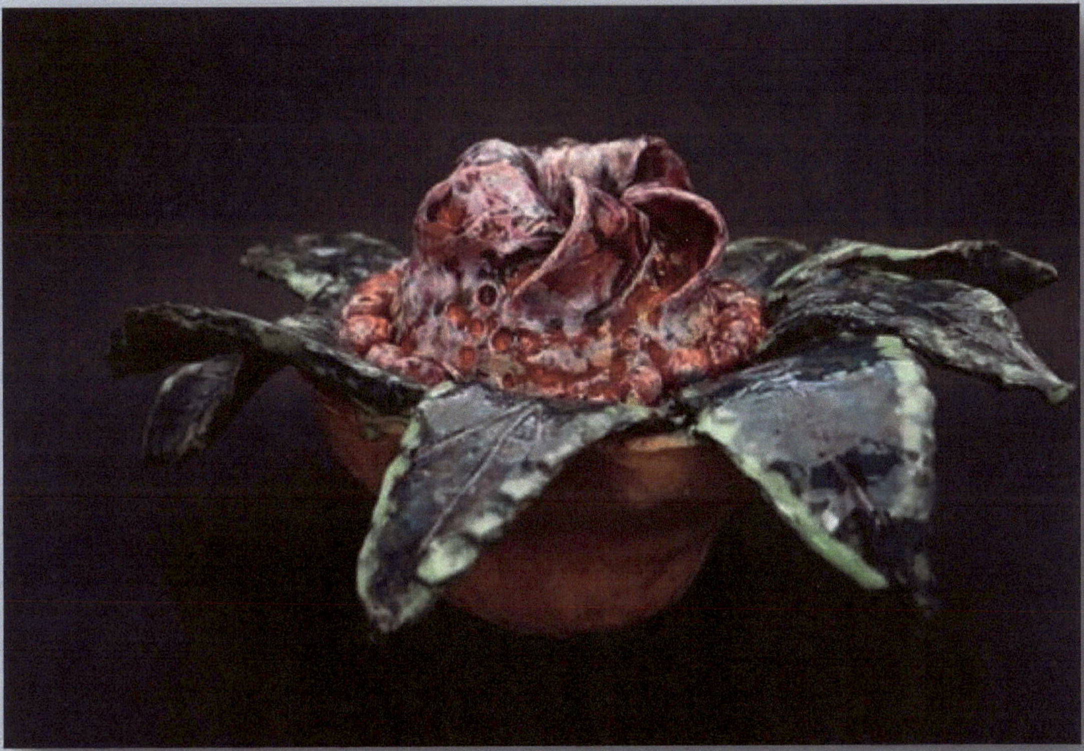

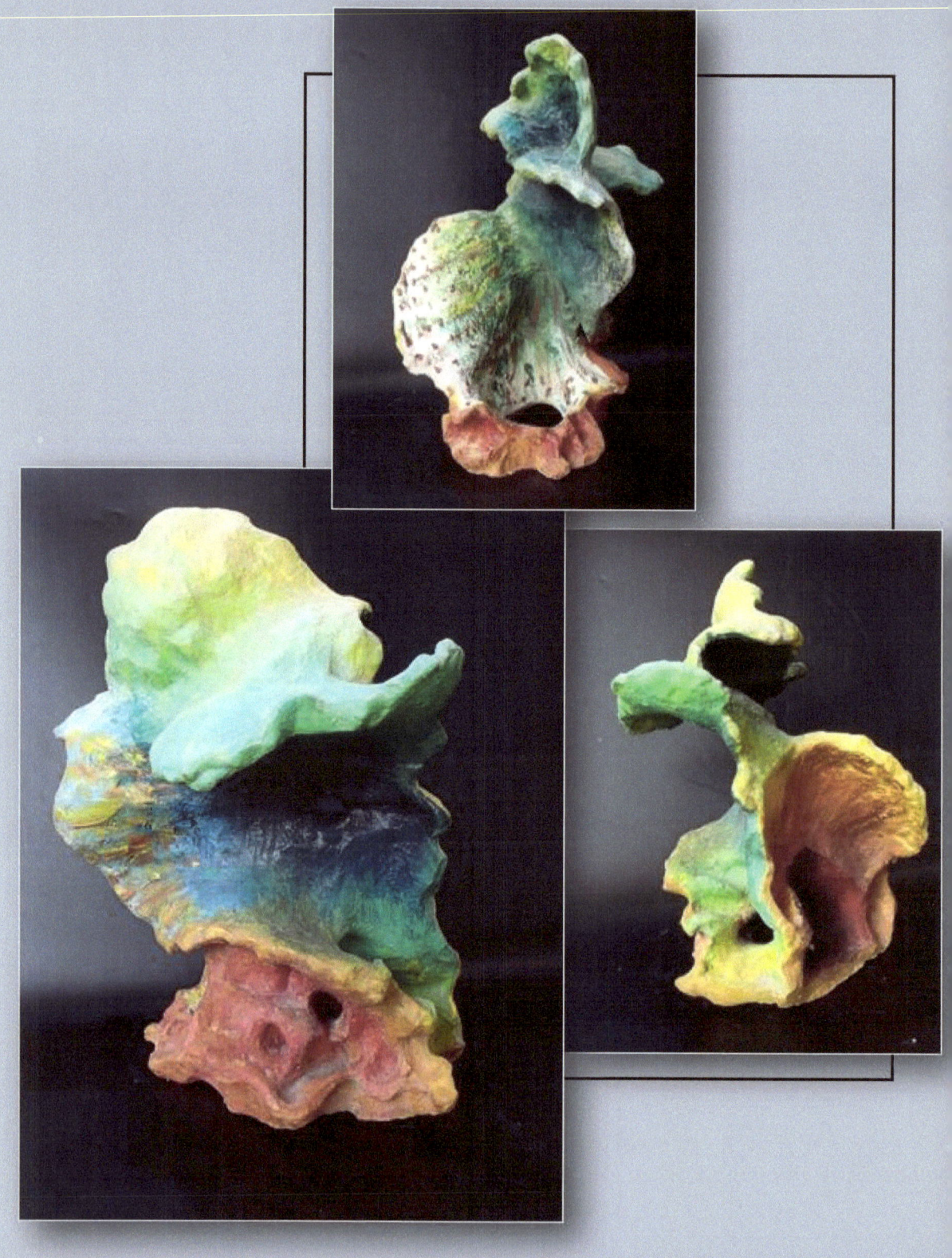

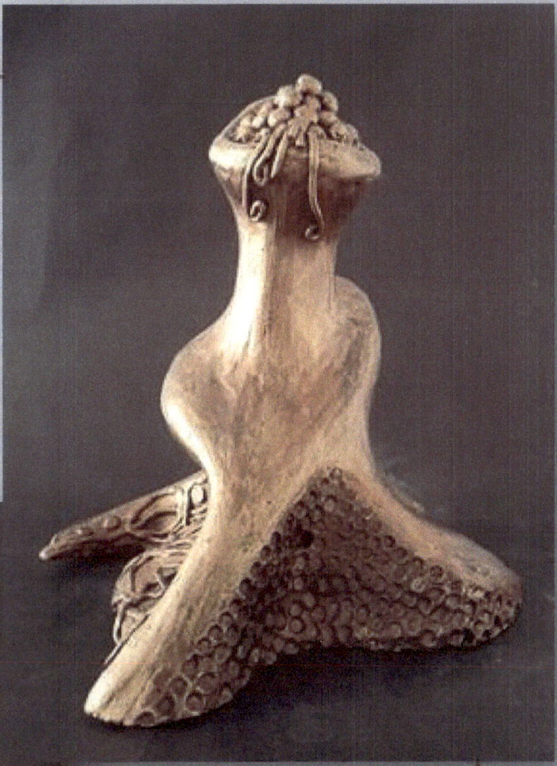

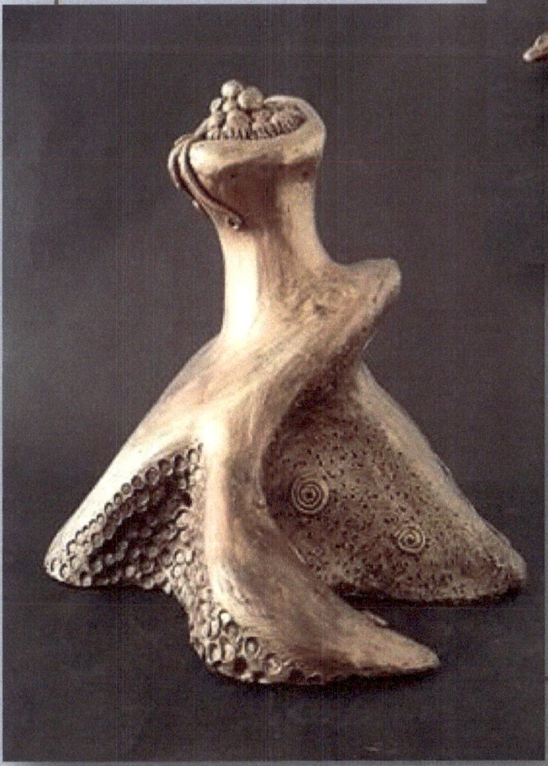

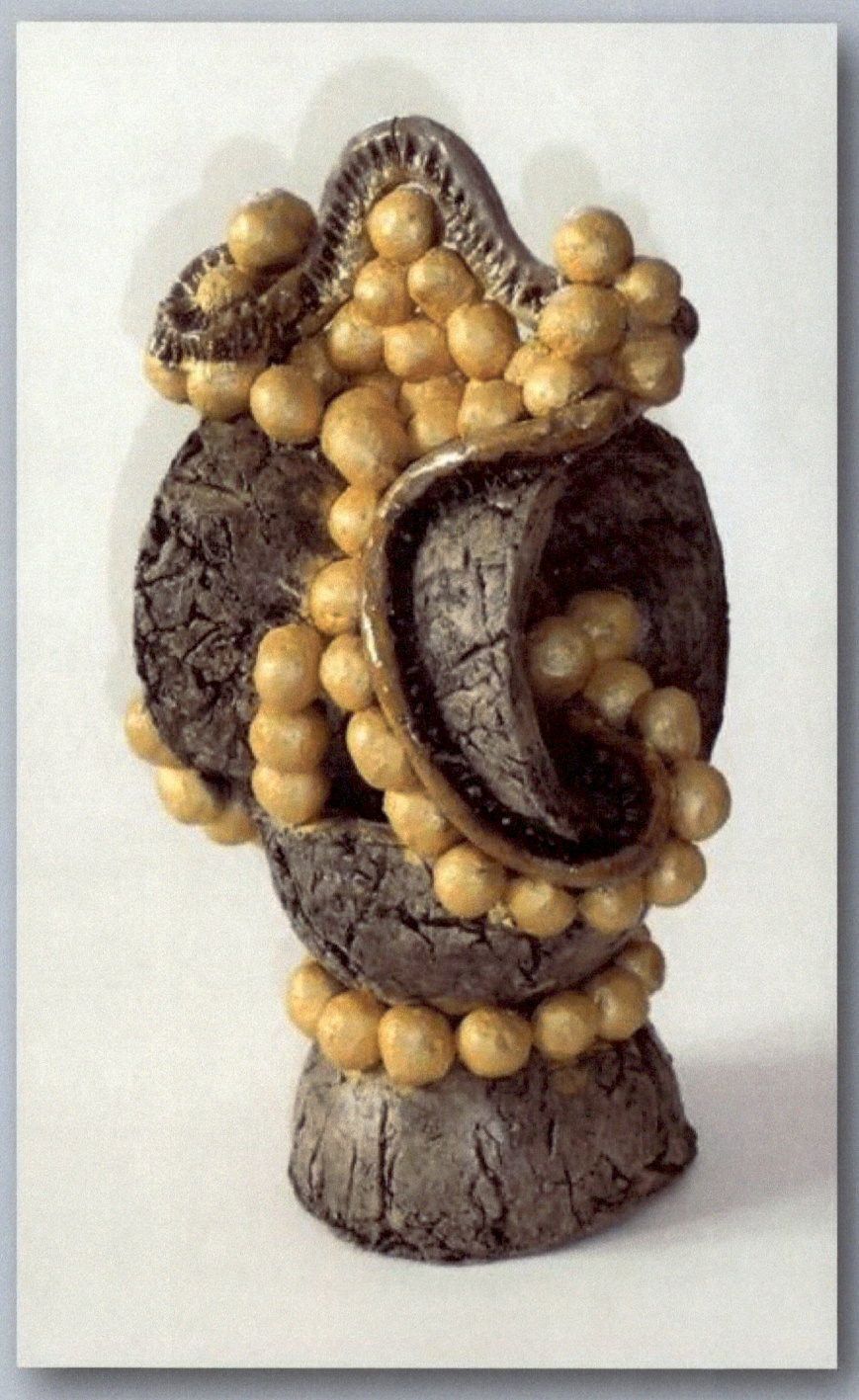

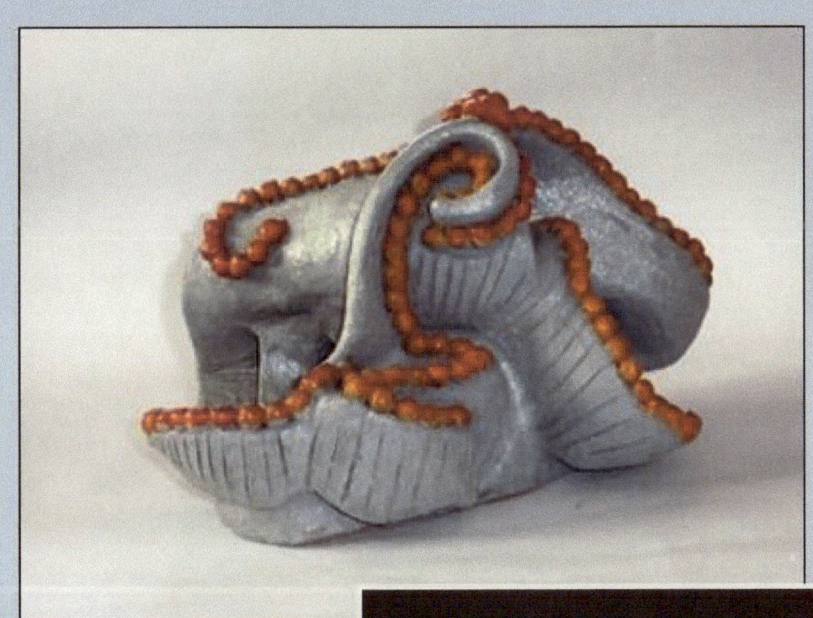
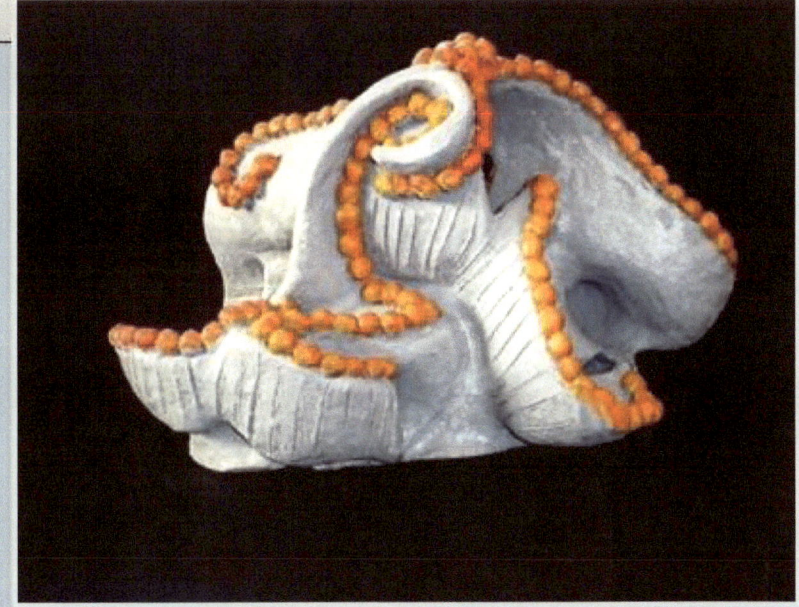

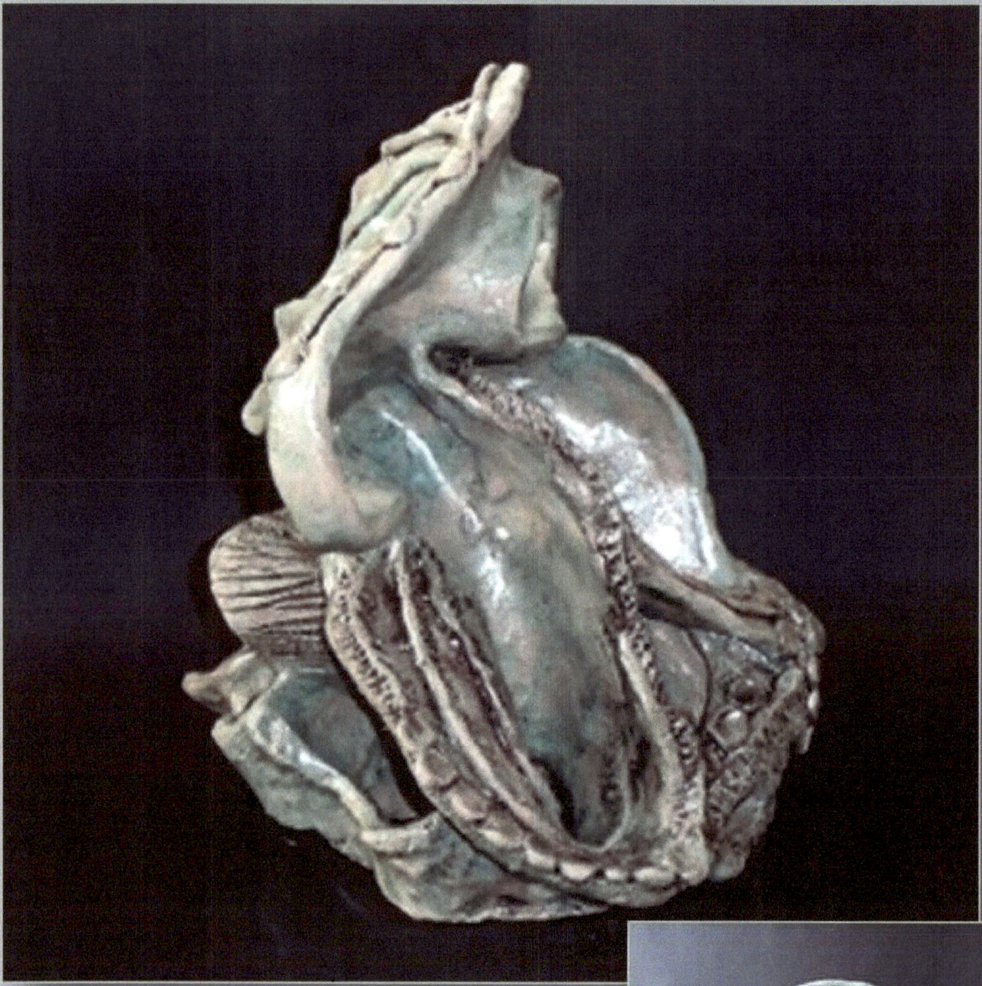

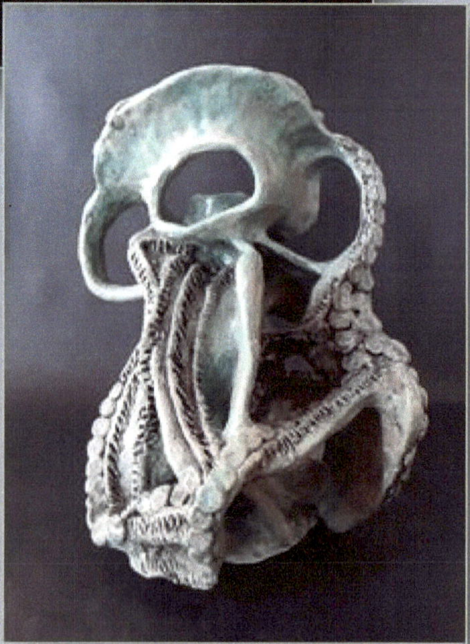

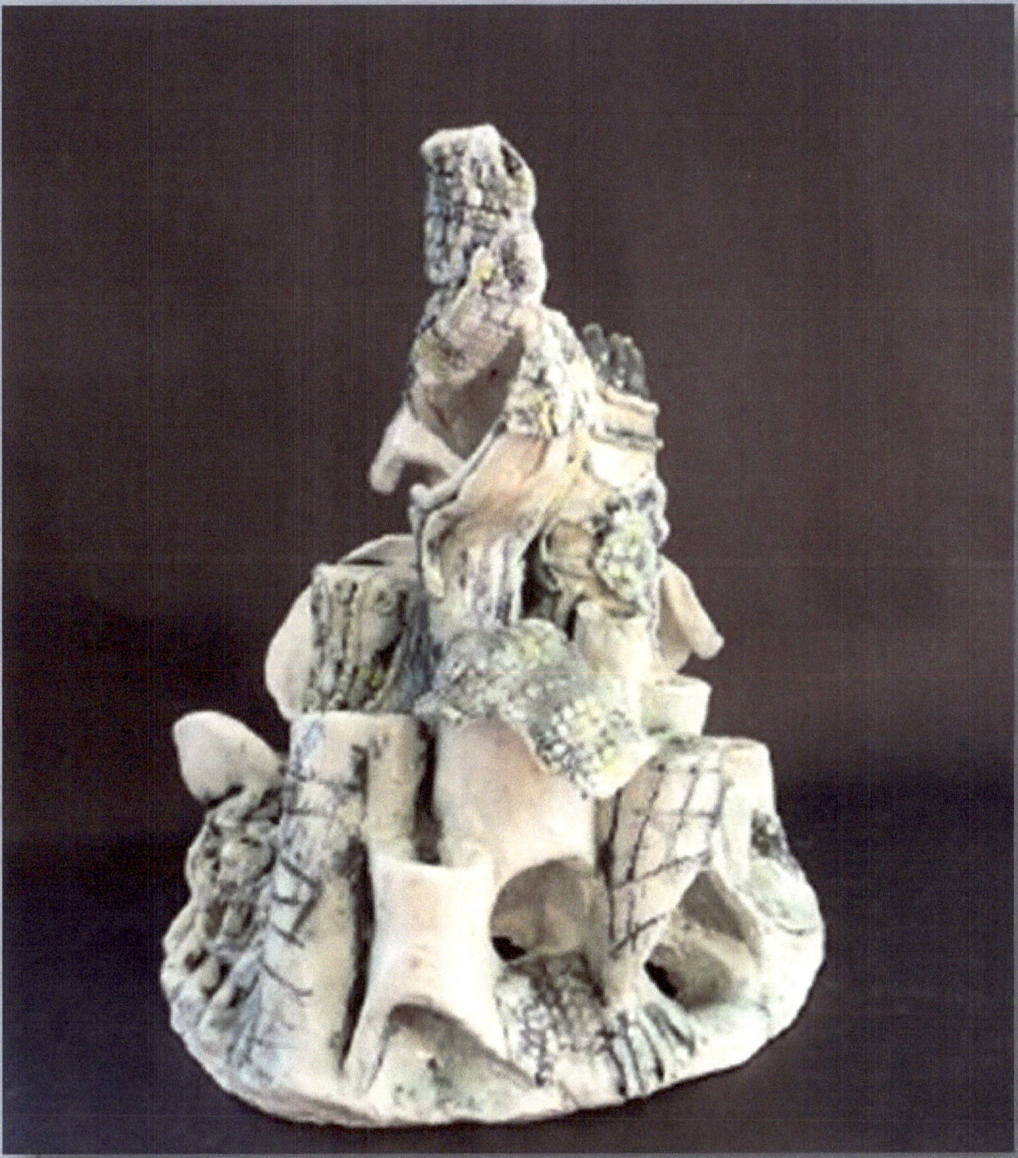

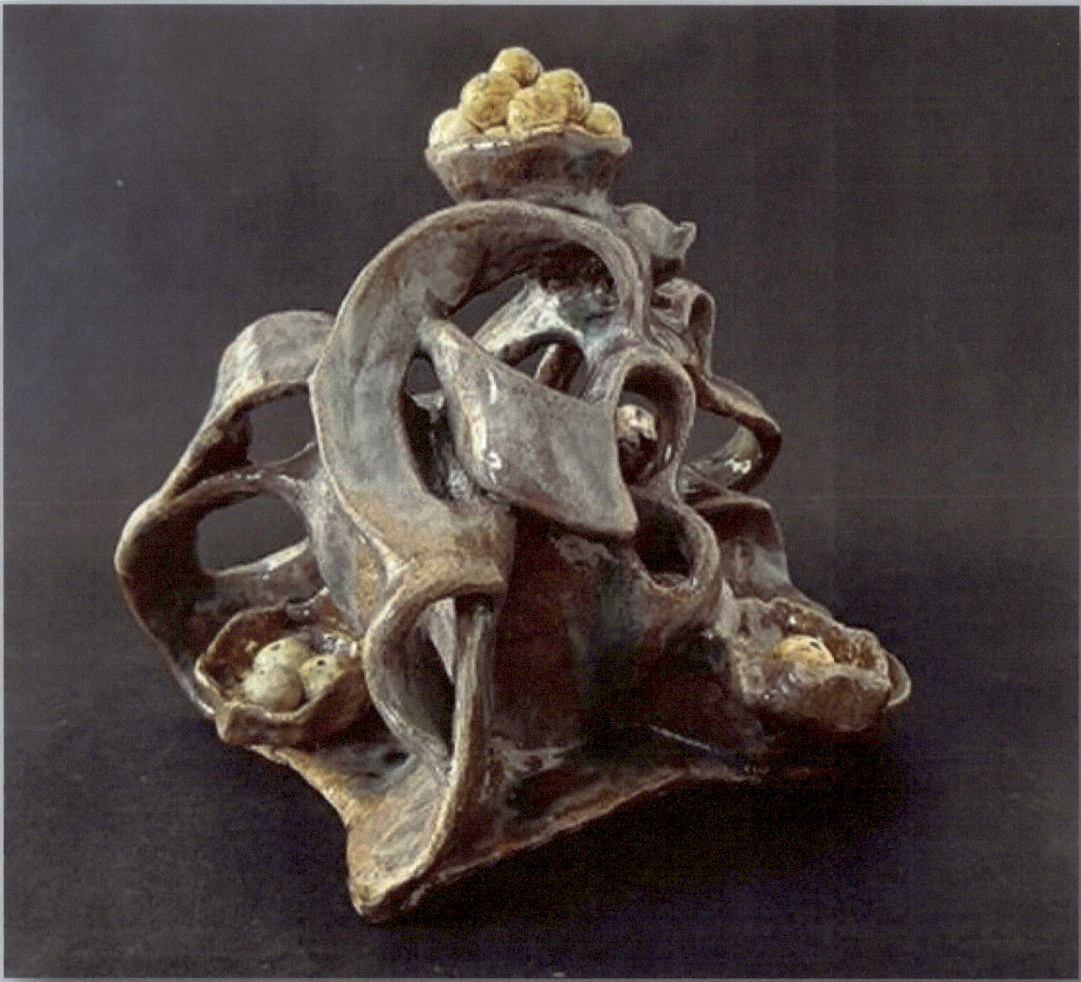

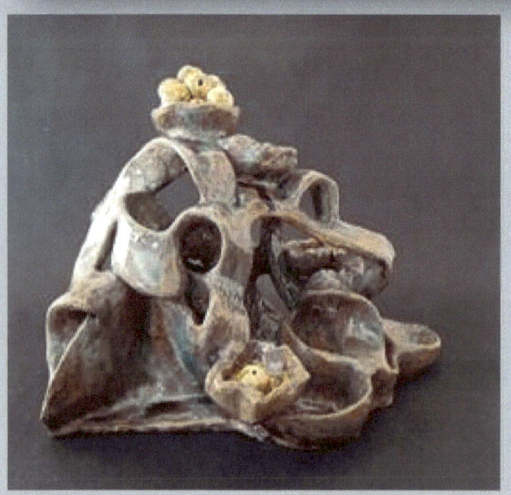
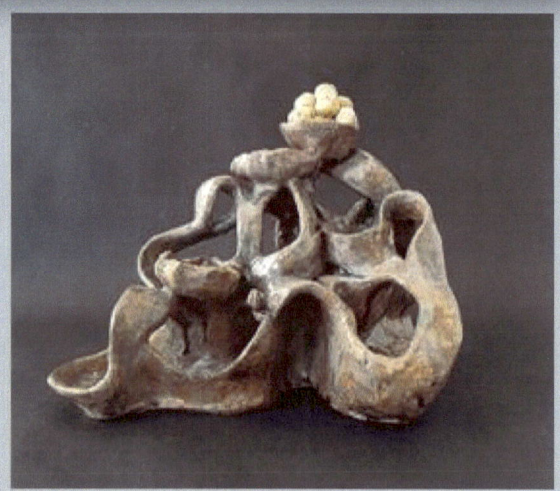

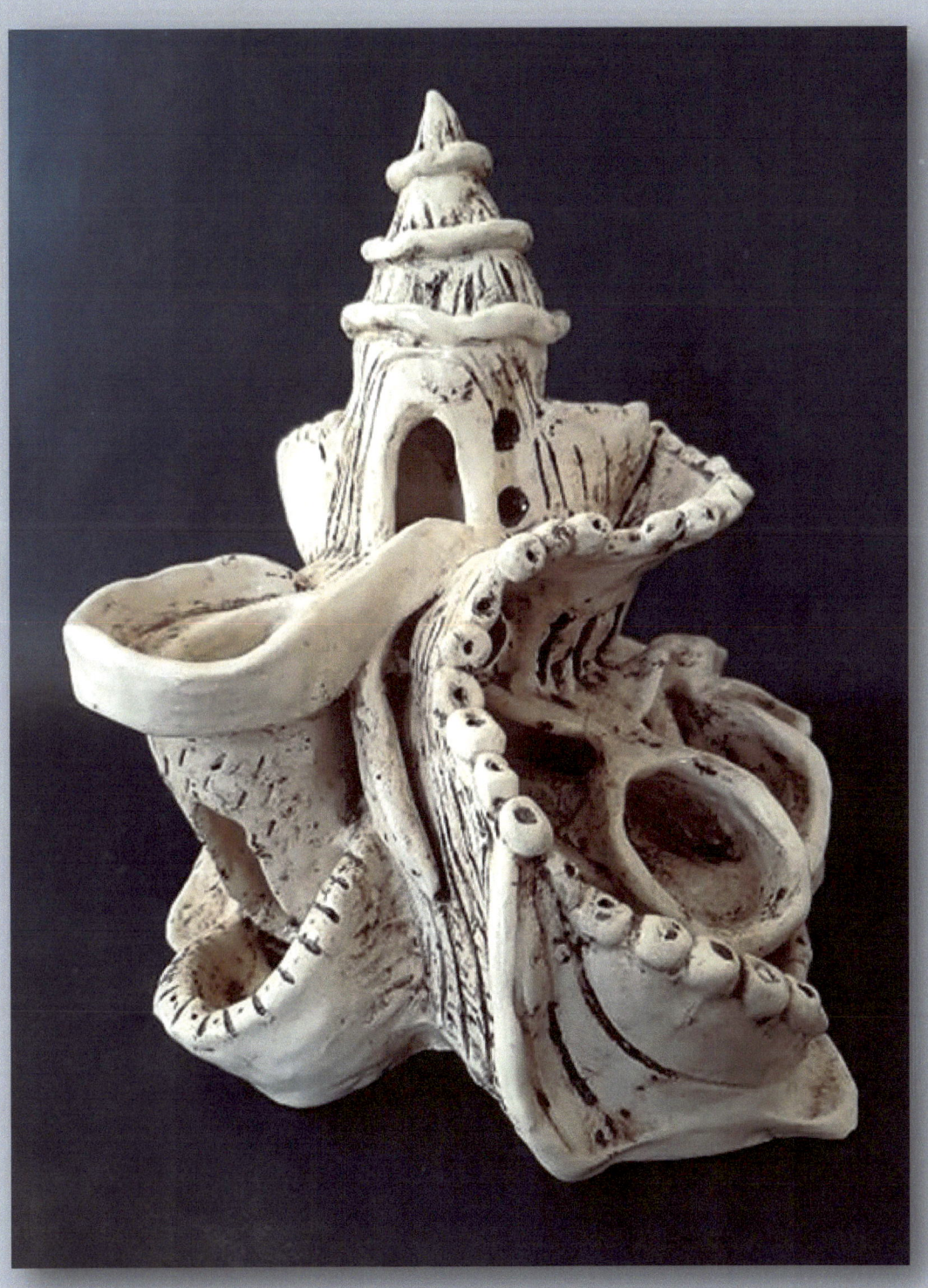

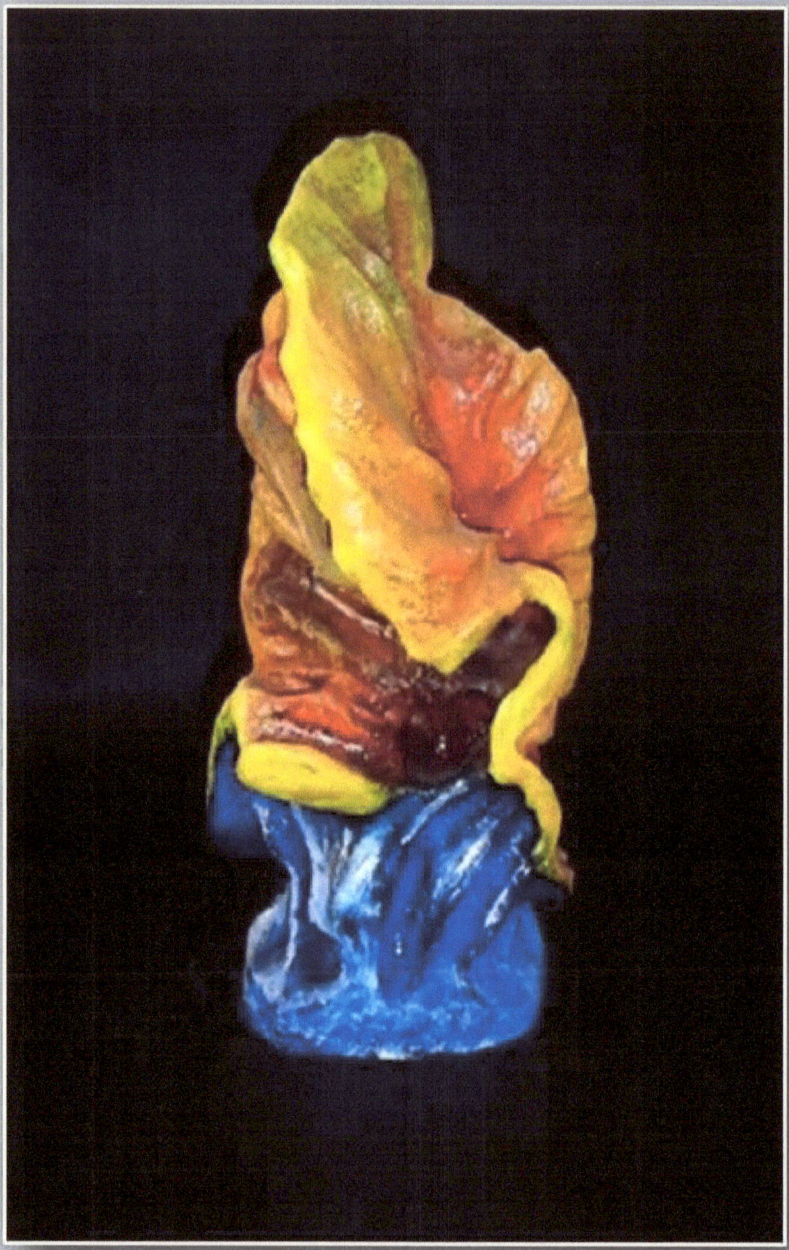

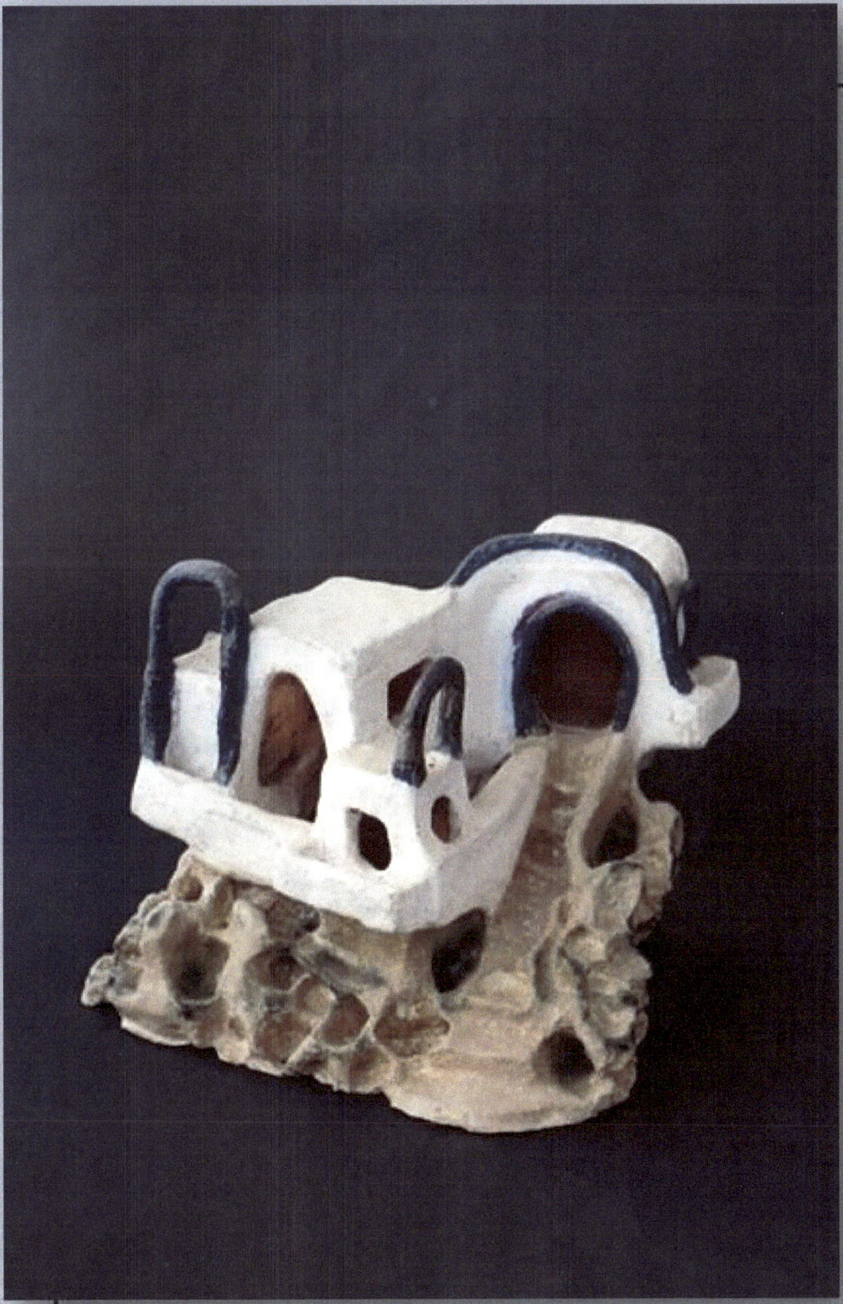

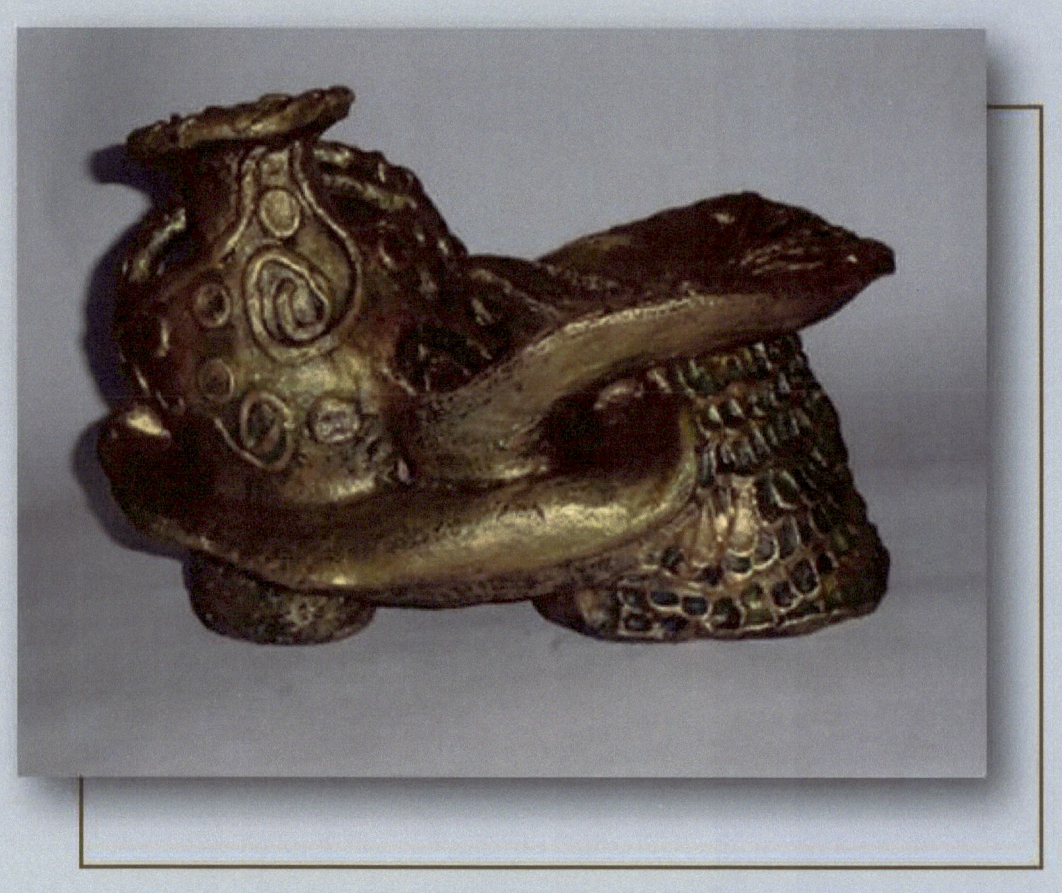

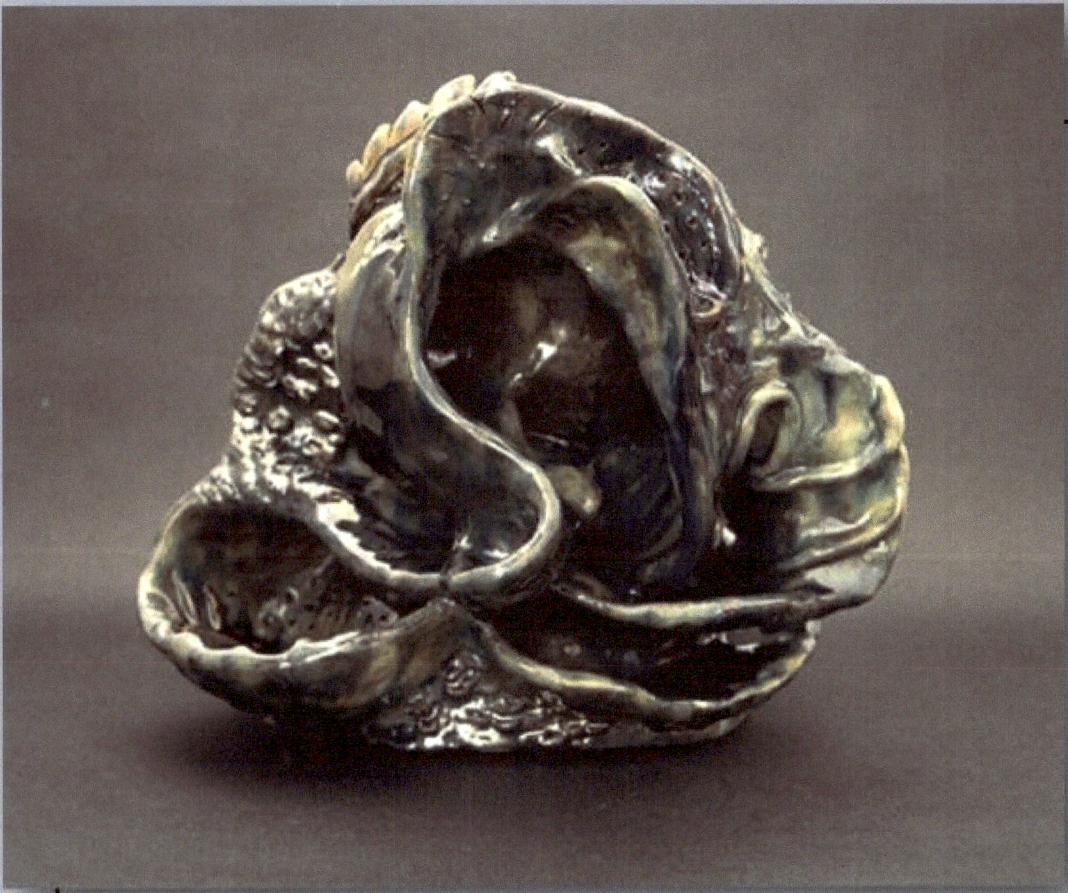

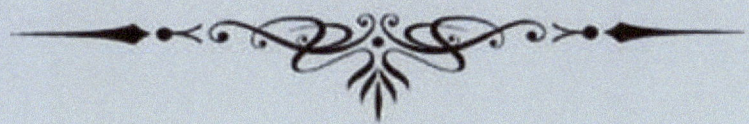

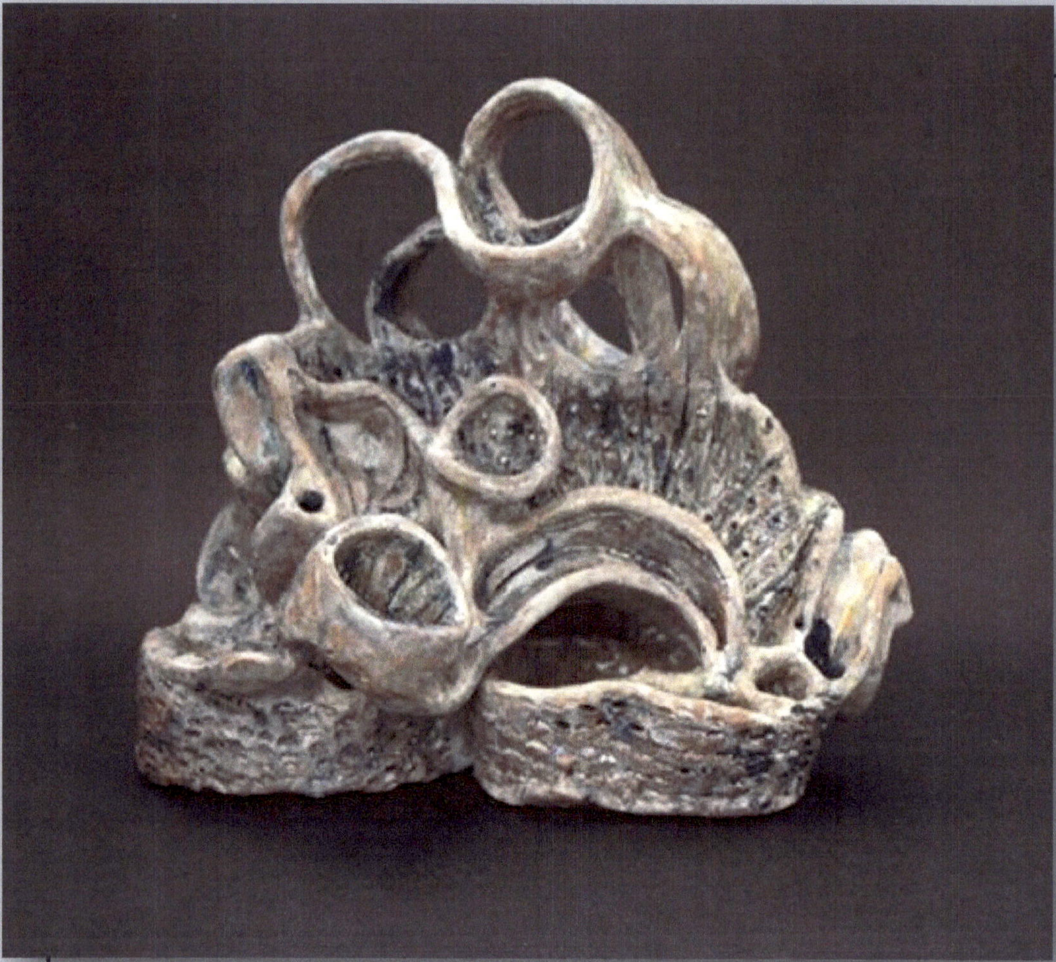

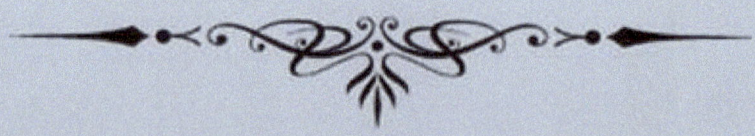

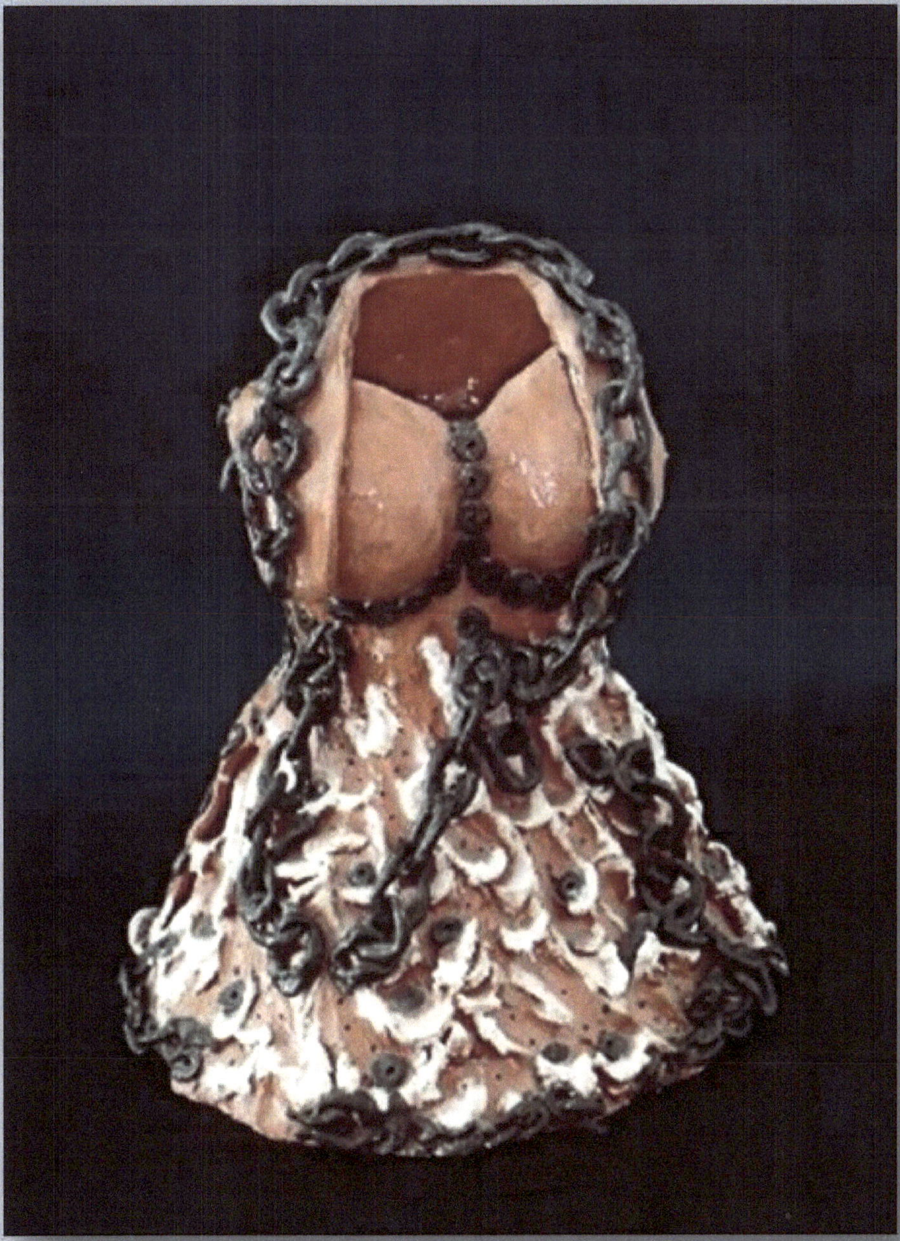

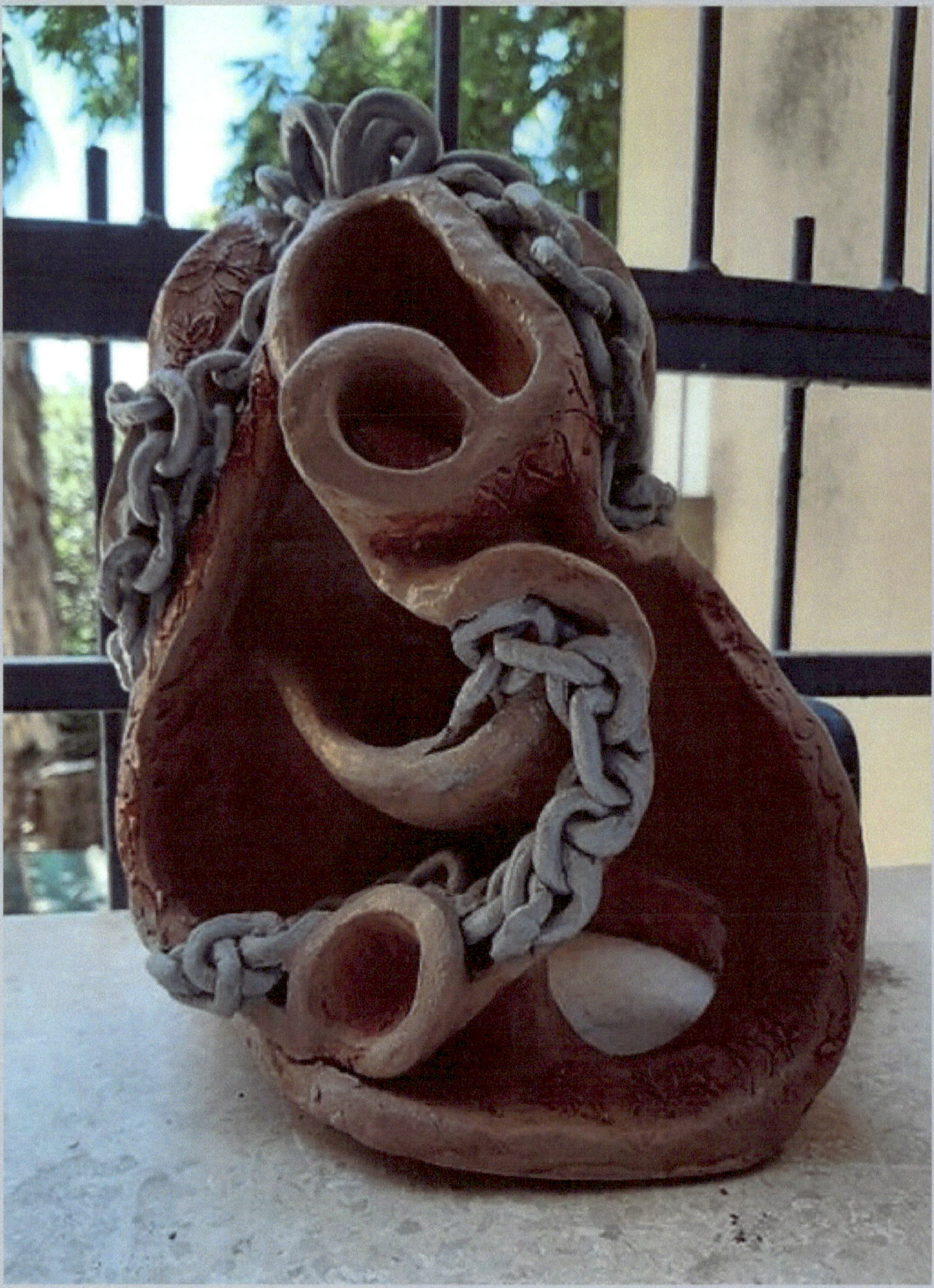

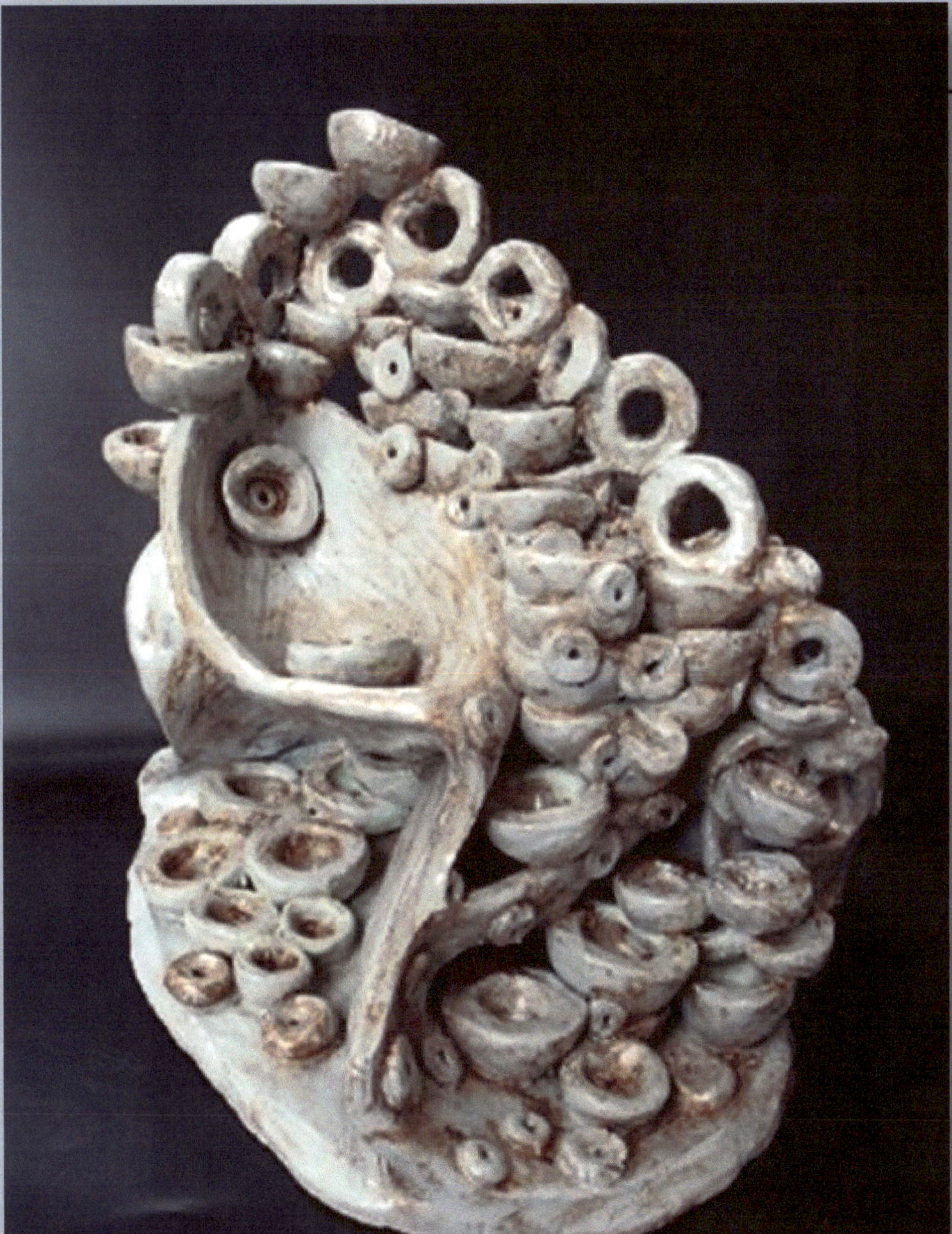

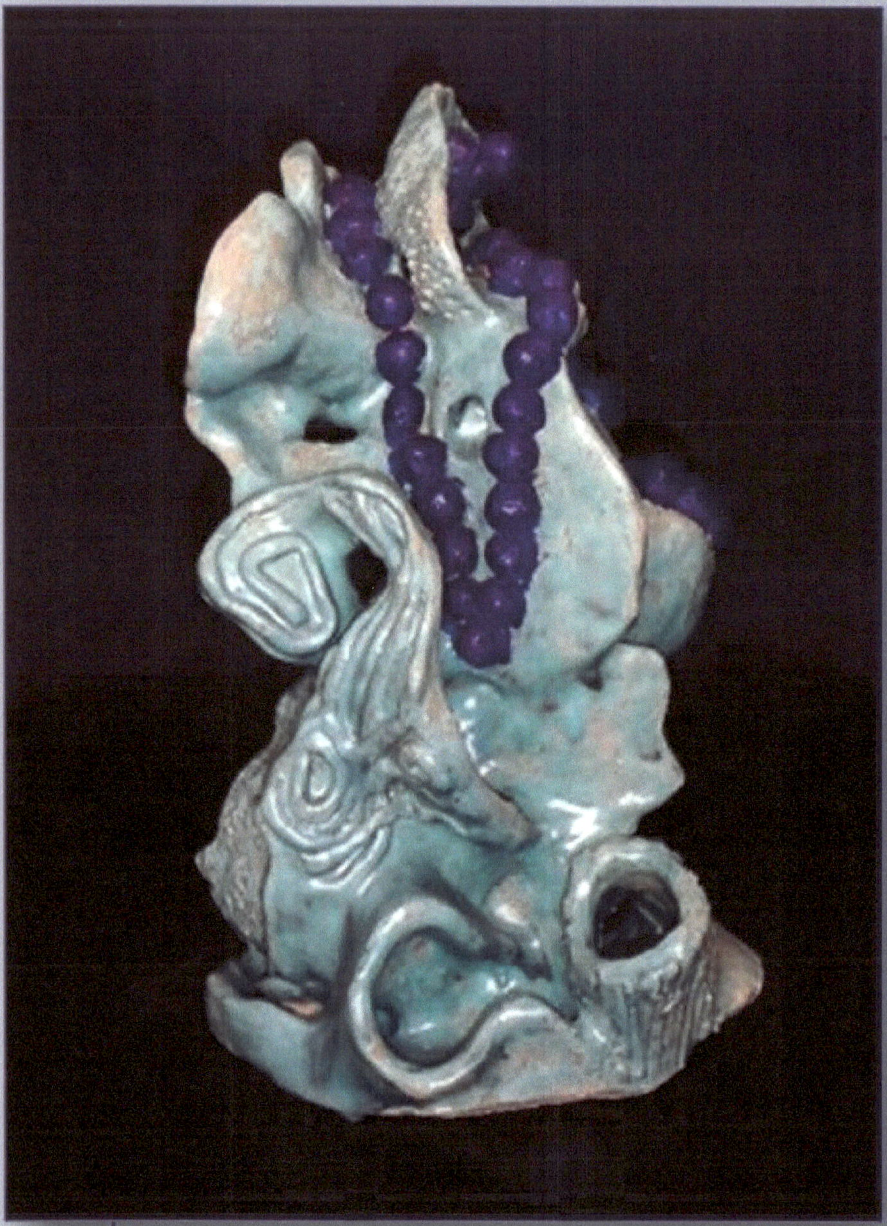

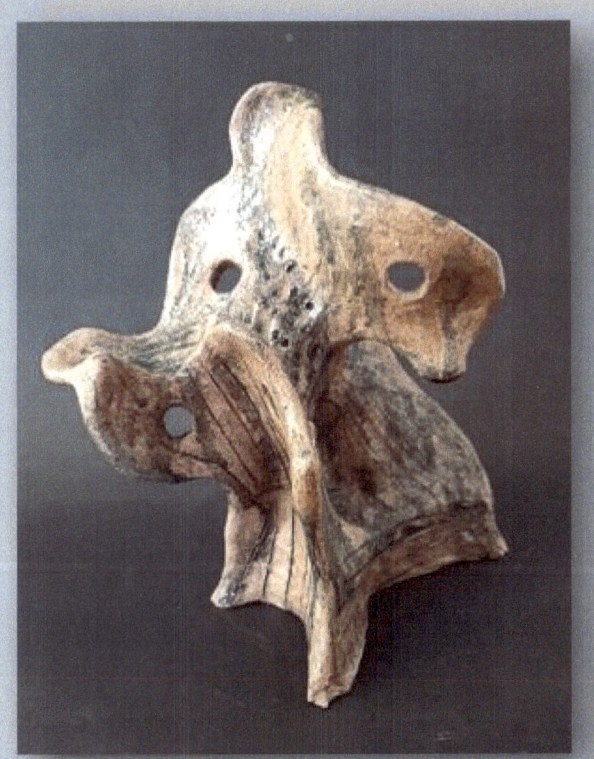 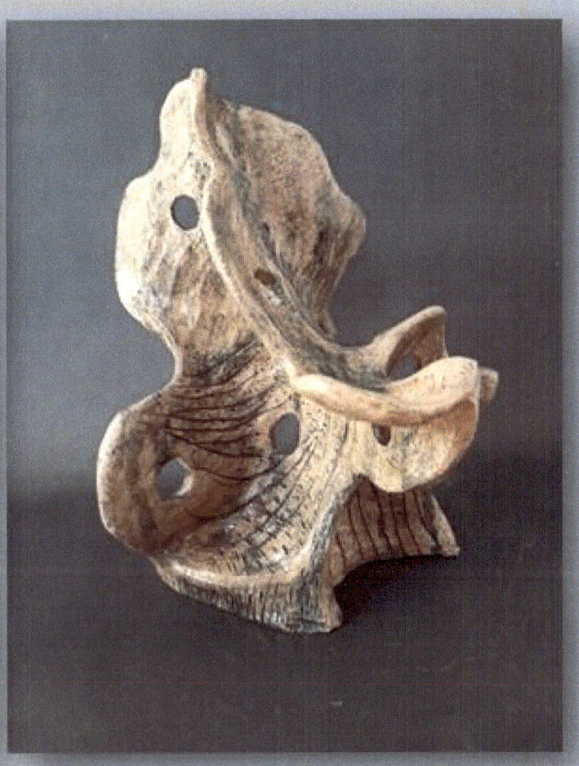

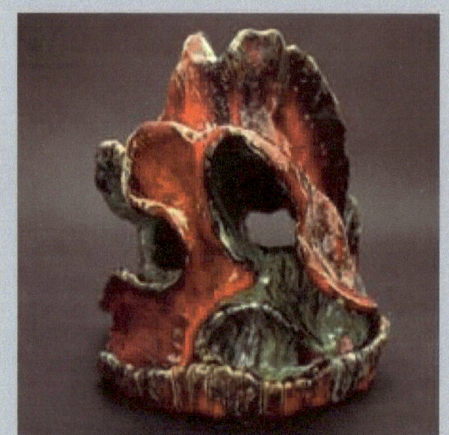
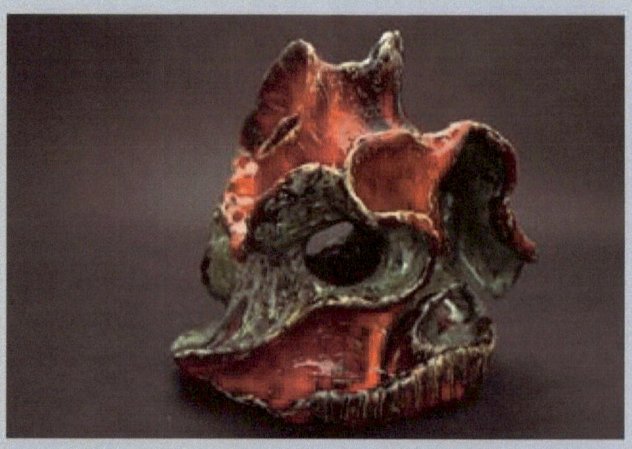
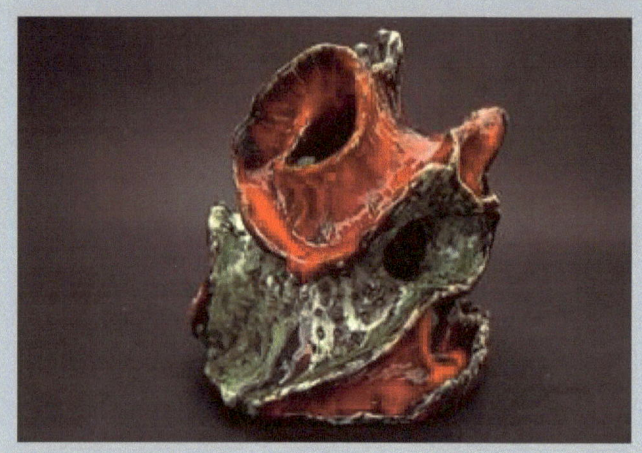
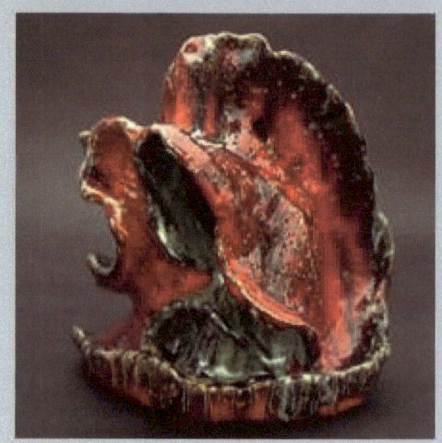

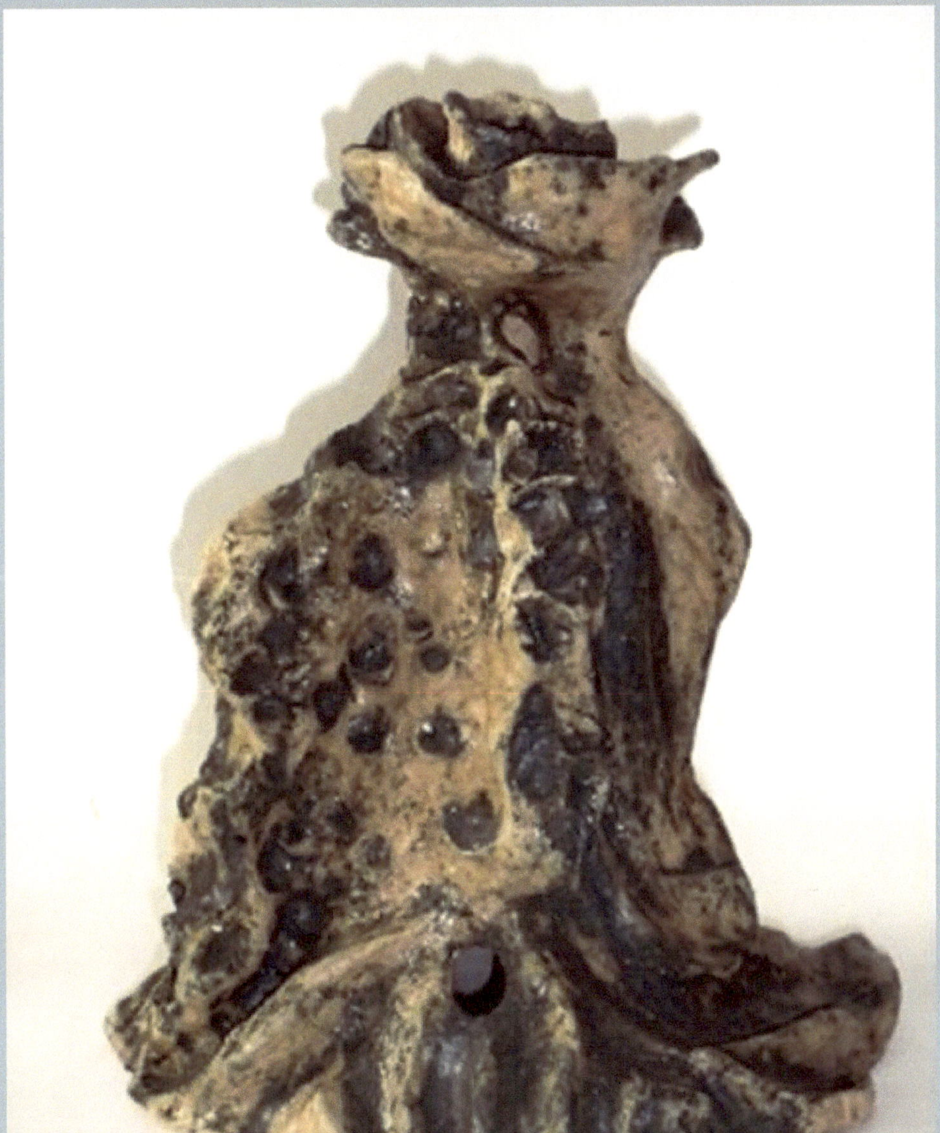

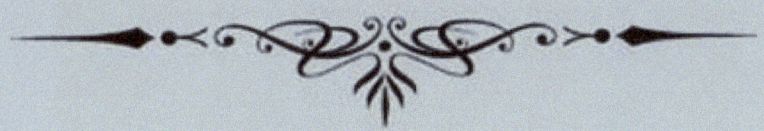

2013

www.ingramcontent.com/pod-product-compliance
Lightning Source LLC
Chambersburg PA
CBHW040454220526
45473CB00004B/1630

9798717918251